Based on the wildly popular business training seminar

Organizational Strategies
for the
Overwhelmed

How to Manage Your Time, Space, & Priorities

to Work Smart, Get Results, & Be Happy

Organizational Strategies for the Overwhelmed

Written by: JoAnn R. Corley

To order this book visit www.joanncorley.com

Library of Congress Cataloging –in– Publications available upon
request.

ISBN: 1466481412

📖 Table of Contents

Introduction

Section 1: The "Me" in Team is the Me In Time

Section 2: Managing Space & Stuff

Section 3: Managing Information

Section 4: Managing Time, Priorities & Takes

Introduction

Laying the Foundation
Are You Overwhelmed?

"We must become stronger

than our circumstances."

Introduction

Laying the Foundation - Are You Overwhelmed?

I have the great opportunity to travel all over North America, conducting a variety of professional development workshops. One of the most popular is entitled, *Organizational Skills for the Overwhelmed.* Isn't that a great title! It truly expresses what the attendees in my seminars feel.

Why? Many in my seminars express how a colleague has been laid off and now they not only have their current job responsibilities, but their former colleague's as well. Additionally, budget cuts continue as well as resistance to new hiring.

Welcome to the "the new normal." What is the new normal? The new normal is the ever-evolving scope and fluency of job responsibilities.

I truly believe that in light of this new normal, a new set of employee competencies must be developed to thrive and succeed. One of which is effectively managing ever-changing responsibilities and workload in the context of time, priorities, and the flow of information that floods our workspace. And with that, *still* be able to deliver results - get the right things done at the right time.

And that's where the feeling of overwhelm enters the picture. Overwhelm is an emotional response that is triggered when your brain gets a signal that too much is going on for you to reasonably process and thereby threatens the desire and possibility of getting things done in a way you think you should.

In fact, the deeper emotion in play is commonly fear because your brain perceives, "too much stuff, to much to do, going on, expected." That then challenges your sense of confidence to be a responsible, competent team member. You're ultimately afraid that you'll fail – won't meet the expectations – failure looms.

In fact three key descriptive words in the definition of overwhelm are submerge, overcome, and overpower. The definition continues: to overcome by superior force or numbers, to overpower in thought or feeling.

The Remedy to Overwhelm

The critical overriding remedy to succeed in the battle against overwhelm is to work from a two prong approach. The first is to skillfully manage yourself and your reactions to the chaos of the day, the flood of information, and all the unforeseen craziness. In essence start with managing yourself on the inside.

The second is to more effectively manage what's going on on the outside for as much as you have control over. **It's an inside – out approach.**

The information provided in this book will help you do this. You'll find practical strategies, tips, and insights. You'll gain greater insight into how and why you and others operate the way they do - both at work and home. It all will help you work smarter, get better results while reducing overwhelm and stress.

Learning to Work Smart is Critical

The ability to work smart in the 21st century workplace really matters! That ability impacts your confidence, level of stress, career success, personal life…and more.

As a career and management coach, those are compelling needs and there in lies the motivation to release this book.

It's written from the view of a coach – someone who wants to help someone get results. So it contains practical, immediately actionable principles, strategies, and how-tos on how to manage time better, determine priorities, effectively organize stuff, among other things. It is based on a popular seminar and has been delivered to thousands across North America.

This is not a "typical" time management - how to get organized book. As I've delivered the seminar that inspired this book throughout the past few years, deeper themes have emerged surrounding what would be considered a "general topic."

Those themes and corresponding content are being presented in this book. Themes such as: strategic thinking, decision making, the role of emotions, life management, boundaries, personality drivers, personal philosophies about time and understanding behavior, to name a few.

When you think about it, if not effectively managed all of those can contribute to a constant state of overwhelm and negative stress.

Including all those themes is why this is not just another time management or how to get organized book and is worth your time and investment. It is broader in scope and thereby of greater value.

Also there is dual value in that they are relevant to both your personal and professional life.

In The End What Really Matters?...
Your Health & Happiness

One of the key objectives in being a career coach is helping my clients attain a meaningful level of happiness and satisfaction in their work life.

In this ever changing economic climate, coupled with the ebb and flow of job responsibilities that in some cases are an on-going moving target, happiness and satisfaction become moving targets as well.

I do believe that in having practical - meaningful tools, techniques, and strategies that enable you to work smarter and feel more capable and confident, you can attain a greater level of happiness and satisfaction in your work in spite of ongoing volatility. And this, believe it or not, can impact the quality of your health.

To do that you'll need to exert more control where you can, think smarter (smarter meaning in a more informed, strategic way) about what you're doing, how you're going about your day, and be more thoughtful about the results you really want. This book will help you do that as well.

Additionally, this book - **and this is a critical point** - is designed to help you see the limits of time, being human, and your work culture.

I believe that one key component to being happy in and at work is *confidently* knowing you are doing the best you can in the context of reality.

That's why taking to heart this next section is so important.

God grant me the serenity
to accept the things I cannot change;
courage to change the things I can;
and wisdom to know the difference.

- commonly known as The Serenity Prayer

How to Approach & Use the Information in This Book

Since this book is derived from a seminar I deliver, at times it may sound and read like you're in one. I didn't want to completely edit out that feel as you read through the content. That's why you won't find chapters as in a traditional book, rather sections. The sections represent the modules of the seminar.

In all of my seminars, I start with an overriding philosophy and I recommend the same for you the reader.

Have this frame of mind...

1. Stay Grounded in Reality – Focus on What You Can Influence & Control

Whenever you approach a topic of this nature, stay grounded in reality. In reading this book, there will be situations in your home or work life that you'll be asked to consider. Some aspect of those situations you may not be able to change – that you in fact have no control over.

Ex: You are dealing with and frustrated with constant interruptions and yet your job is being a receptionist in a busy office.

> The key philosophy going forward: focus on what you have *complete control* over and what you can *influence*. Let go of and don't focus on the things you have no control over.

Are there parts of how you handle a situation that you could change?...perhaps. Are there parts of your company culture, team culture, boss's personality or leadership style, job description that can't be changed?...that's possible and in some cases can't and won,t.

Are there elements of these things that you might be able to influence?...perhaps. It's important going forward that you thoughtfully weigh these questions, so you can become clear on what you want to focus on and how you want to channel your precious energy.

2. Approach Everything in Small Bites – Keep it Simple!

I say when I teach *Organizational Skills for the Overwhelmed,* "My goal is not to overwhelm you" (which usually gets a laugh).

I say that because there will be a lot of ideas and "ah has" on what to address and you'll be saying to yourself, "Oh my gosh, where do I start?"

How do you build a brick building?...one brick at a time. So the easiest, least overwhelming, most successful approach to using this material is to start with just one-small thing and stick with it long enough to see meaningful progress.

3. Find Your 1%

The key benefit about starting small is doing the same small thing really does make progress – in fact substantial progress.

Consider this: If you can improve by 1% a day, you can double your effectiveness in 70 days. That's called **the 1% edge**.

So throughout the remainder of the book, as you consider what principles or how-tos you'll put into practice, set yourself up for success by having realistic expectations and attempting things in small bites. Just find your 1%.

In fact the expanded version of the 1% principle is this, *"A little bit done consistently goes a long way."* The key word in this principle is consistent. Consider the fact that many people don't accomplish very much because they are not consistent.

4. Don't' get hung up on the "T's" – Tools, Technology, Tips

Get too hung up on these and it will defeat the purpose of using them!

Ever heard the tip don't touch a piece of paper more than once?... are you kidding! I've met people in my seminars that stress themselves trying to honor that kind of tip. Not helpful!

Even with technology, not all usage of technology translates into time saving efficiency. In some cases, it's quite the opposite.

Bottom line - rules should not rule you...and technology should not either. Who's the boss here - you or it?

As a productivity coach and time management strategist, I'd rather call them guidelines. In fact the most useful way to approach this topic is with the following thoughts:

- Guidelines are just that - to guide you to get more of what you want.

- Practice the principles and apply them in a customized fashion to your style of work and thinking.

- Principles reign over tools. (For example, using a master list is a principle. How one keeps and maintains one can be done in a variety of ways...e.g. a spiral notebook, Outlook task section, visual whiteboard).

- Being aware of your natural work style and thinking style plays a critical role in what will work best for you.

- Ultimately each person needs to develop their own style and systems, which really ends up being a tailored combination of many principles, tools, and techniques.

- If something is working for you, keep doing it or using it!

A Few Final Notes

Why Another "Time Management" Book?

If you were to do a time management or a how to get more organized search on Amazon, you'd find a plethora of books on those topics to purchase. So one would ask, "why add one more book to the mix?"

My reasons are listed below and include my personal wish list when reading a book.

1. I believe there is critical information missing from many of them.

Not that I've read them all, but I've read enough and taught enough seminars across North America to discover that they follow a general style of delivery and cover a general set of content.

Many are based on sharing tips, tricks and techniques on how to manage time and priorities or how to organize your space and stuff. *And yet*, **the ability** to actually execute those tips and techniques is not really addressed. In fact there is rarely a discussion on what precedes the execution, and /or what drives or influences one's ability to do so. **What precedes all those tips and tricks?...decision-making and choices.**

With that in mind, every tip, technique, or principle in this book must be supported with ability to put into practice what's been learned.

Additionally, effective decision-making is key to implementation. That's why the first section of the book is entitled, *"The Me in Time."*

2. Access to the author via coaching or a live seminar

There have been times after reading a book that I would have loved to connect with the author and gotten more customized input. I would have loved to have gotten help matching my real-time experience with the theory and "how-tos" described in the book...in essence gotten real-time coaching or advice.

> **The Key Point** – any person who reads a "how-to" book must within themselves have the power to execute what's being learned. I can teach a group all day about being assertive, as an example, but if the folks hearing the techniques or strategies continually allow themselves to be controlled by fear, the likelihood of implementing what they've learned is minimal at best.

In light of the point mentioned earlier, access to coaching in some cases is really the better approach vs. reading another book or taking a class. In fact in many cases it can save time and money. So readers will have access to me.

Additionally, since this book is based on a popularly delivered seminar, this book can be brought on site to any organization or presented at an event in a variety of modified formats.

3. Social Media provides access to value added content and reader interaction

And finally, it would have been helpful to have the book be on-going and interactive as I sought to apply what I was learning.

In the past that would have been tough to do and really hasn't been part of a "book business model."

But luckily for readers, advances in technology have changed all that. With the birth of blogs and social media, a book can come alive, be a social water cooler, a starting point and on-going source surrounding a topic. The Internet now provides easy access to an expanded experience with the material.

That's my plan for this book. You'll be able to participate in a blog or experience webinars on complimentary topics, as well as connect via various social media channels. It's the 21st century approach to book publishing.

To participate in an on-going experience with the information in this book you can go to www.the1percentedge.com. There you can contact me, read complimentary posts and comments, and get help and support when and where you need it or bring a seminar to your organization.

In summary, I'm confident you'll find the information in this book not typically found in a traditional time management or how to get organized book and you'll have access to the author!

Section 1

The "Me" in Team
is the
Me in Time

"There is a me in team."

-Michael Jordan

Your performance as a team member is embedded in how you use your time and other's time as well.

Managing Time - Being More Organized
The Bigger Picture

I love when I walk into a space and I can breath. Everything is in its place and in a moment, I can find what I'm looking for. Oh joy!

In that simple scenario, being able to find something quickly with ease does not add stress to an already challenging day and so in that there is value. Yet, when you look at the bigger picture – what's the point?

I believe the bigger picture or purpose is *getting the right results*. It's you demonstrating capacity and the capability to manage the elements of a workday to get what you (and dare I say your boss) want!

These days, it is all about productivity and results. Keeping your performance/professional edge in an ever-increasing competitive performance market is critical. At the time of this writing, there are lots of talented, skilled unemployed people ready to take *your* spot.

As a career management coach, I'm here to tell you - you are in a performance market. What does that mean? *Everyday* your performance in some way impacts a potential decision to keep you or let you go. As one of my seminar attendees so aptly proclaimed, "Every day is a job interview."

"It's not a job market, but a performance market."

Performance at work is webbed in time, choosing priorities, finding things, execution, collaborating with colleagues, managing information; and all of that needs to be skillfully managed to get the right results.

With that in mind, something as simple as managing email more effectively, locating a file or documents faster helps you move more quickly towards the targeted results for the day and although subtle, cumulatively can impact the bigger picture.

All those efforts to be organized, or using the latest time management tool, technique, or technology is really for the ultimate purpose of helping you execute work to get the right results at the right time…to have your personal and professional life turn out a certain kind of way – to get what you want.

So let's say this – this book is not so much about time management and how to get organized, but is about…

- √ staying employed
- √ mastering your performance
- √ being a stand out
- √ being raise worthy
- √ developing 21st century workplace competencies
- √ feeling more confident in handling fluid job responsibilities
- √ reducing your stress

And I bet you could name more!

Results Clarified

"Results are the building blocks of your life...so make sure the ones you get are the ones you want."

In the introduction the essential focus on results was introduced. To drive home this critical point, a clarification must be made.

Have you ever known someone who just seems to be super busy all the time?

I bet you'd venture to say that if someone is busy they are getting results right? The answer is yes.

Actions produce results.

In fact actions of any kind will produce a result - **behaviors always produce results** - they just may not be the results you really wanted or initially intended.

Being busy, therefore, can sometimes be an illusion to the ultimate goal of getting targeted results (the right things done at the right time). Busy can even feel good and can keep you going in the direction that ultimately may not be what you really want.

In fact when you think about it, busy doesn't necessarily translate into getting the "needed or desired" things done and yet, busy can even feel good.

So in the spirit of making this universal law work for you, you must take the time to identify exactly what results you really want.

At work ask yourself, "What results do I want from this day vs. what's on my to-do list" (more on the "to-do" list later).

A result has a different feel and mindset than a to-do.

Career Success Tip:
Quantitate your work for reviews and résumés. Put percentages and numbers to what you accomplish.

The follow-up questions then are, " How does my use of time match that?"

"Is it time for a revised approach?…an updated career management or performance plan at work?"

Career management you say? **Yes, the results you get in a day of work translates into your performance, which turns into a composite of your career.**

On a larger scale, each result is a building block being laid now, which ultimately creates the future.

Can you safely say then … that determining the results you want in certain life contexts is really a form of life management and therefore, time management is ultimately life management?

I say absolutely! That's why the next section carries an essential point in moving forward.

To Get Results – You've Got To Be a Skilled Manager

"Those who are the most successful are very skilled at managing their own lives."

In order to achieve the necessary outcomes and competencies to generate consistent work life success, you must begin with laying a strong foundation.

Let's begin by considering the word management. I believe in order to get more and better results (with less stress I might add) you must change the way you might traditionally see the word manage.

When I ask this question is my seminars, I get lots of interesting answers, "When you hear the word manage or management, what comes to mind that you can say publically?

Then I ask the question (warning them it is a bit of a trick question), "Is everyone in here a manager today?" Most people say yes and few say no.

What's the right answer? The right answer is yes! Everyone in every one of my seminars is a manager whether they bear the official title or not. The same holds true for the word leader – everyone is a leader whether it's official in the eyes of others or not.

In reality both managing and leading are not necessarily titles, but behaviors. I bet you know people who hold those titles but don't act it.

So YOU are in fact a manager. Let's look at the dictionary's formal definition:

Manage:

"To handle and direct with some degree of skill."

You'll notice the two key action verbs – handle and direct. Both imply a power going out – outward motion or energy.

And what's the qualifier?…with a degree of skill.

What's a skill? It's not just something one knows how to do …but something that one does *well*.

In today's workplace you must develop the skill of managing. In order to do that, you must be able to exert more power than the thing being exerted upon you. Stephen Covey states in *The 7 Habits of Highly Effective People*, "Act or be acted upon."

Consider these statements:

> *Context:* Interruptions

> Somebody is managing somebody. Are they managing you or are you managing them? You also can use the word *lead* in the same question.

Context: Find it difficult to not answer the phone or respond to a text

Who is managing whom? Is the phone managing the person or the person managing the phone?

In those two scenarios you can see how powerful the word manage really is and the essential role it plays in this topic.

In summary, in order to get the kind of results you want, you must be empowered enough to skillfully handle and direct what's going on around you. Another way of putting it – you must be more assertive and strategic with the dynamics of your workday.

Life Success Side Bar

A quality, happy life, I believe is based on one's ability to manage his or her life effectively to get the outcomes or results desired.

For example, someone who manages his or her finances effectively is more likely to have a more quality, happy life.

Someone who manages relationships via healthy boundaries is more likely to have a happy, quality life and so on.

The 7 Manages

I hope you are convinced by now that being a skilled manager is essential to getting the results you want.

And that begs the question…skilled at managing what exactly?

Consider the list below and use it as your checklist. I'll be referring to this list as "THE LIST" throughout the rest of the book.

If you were to ask yourself what are the areas you'd like to get better at managing in relation to the dynamics of a work day, I bet your answer would show up on this list….

Getting results – improving your performance requires effective management of:

1. Yourself
2. Others
3. Time
4. Priorities & Tasks
5. Space & Stuff
6. Information
7. Technology

In reviewing this list, ask yourself these questions, "How skilled am I at managing_____." (You fill in the blank.)

When looking at the outcomes you'd like to get either on a professional or personal level, fill in this statement. "I want to become skilled (or more skilled) at managing _____."

It All Begins With Me

"It's an inside job."

Some people think that managing time better would require nothing more than picking up an organizer or attending the next Franklin-Covey time management class.

Or, being more organized is nothing more than taking a field trip to the local Container Store or storage isle at Walmart, purchasing some boxes and bins and attacking that clutter pile that's been an annoyance for quite some time.

For some people - for those one or two piles - that might work.

However, to consistently and effectively manage piles or time, a fresh look and approach to the common themes of time and organizational management is needed.

There is a ME in time!

Let's start with this basic premise - there is a "me" in time. That me *is* the essential and foundational component to getting results in the 7 Manages.

Though the items on that list are not in any particular order, the #1 item is there on purpose - Managing Myself. Everything else on that list is built on and contingent upon "the me."

So as you begin this section, ask yourself this question, **"How skilled am I at managing myself?"**

You'll find as you continue to read, the answer to that question is the most important one you'll answer and the key to applying the tips and techniques in the remainder of the book.

The "Me" Formula™

All human beings are programmed a certain way both in terms of how they process and interpret their life experience as well as how they're wired in their personality. Both will be examined in this section.

Additionally, you'll see how each impacts your ability to get your desired results and manage "the list."

Review this formula:

$$E \Rightarrow T \Rightarrow F \Rightarrow D \Rightarrow B$$

It reads… E impacts T impacts F impacts D impacts B.

E= Experience or event triggers

T = thoughts that generate

F = feelings that influence and drive

D = decisions which result in

B = behaviors which are the results or outcomes

When human beings encounter an event, have an experience or simply something happens to them, immediately what's triggered is:

a.   a conscious thought process

b. a triggered emotion or reaction usually out of the subconscious recorded from a previous experience.

Though the "Me" formula shows the thoughts first, sometimes the feeling is activated before the conscious thought process. Ever said to yourself, "I don't know why I'm feeling this way?"

By the way, that formula can happen in a millisecond or very slowly – triggered, self-induced and purposely nurtured.

The Source of Thoughts – The "T" in the Me Formula

Your thinking, both on a conscious and/or subconscious level, is a composite of key sources, which I call a personal filter or *personal interpreter*. Everyone has one. How do you know? Two people can have the exact same experience and interpret it in completely different ways.

That interpretation is complied with and from a personal filter and is comprised of these 4 key components:

- Your **personality type** (natural wiring)
- Your **life experience** up until that moment (pre-conditioning)
- The **beliefs** developed by that life experience
- The **values** you hold and that were shaped through that life experience.

Of those listed, the *two major sources are natural wiring and conditioning*.

Here is an explanation of all four.

1. Natural Wiring (Personality)

I use natural wiring as another way of describing personality or temperament. It's a fascinating study, but for our purposes I want to discuss some simple concepts and behaviors regarding personality that impact the **Me Formula**. (By the way, if you've never taken a personality test, I highly recommend you do. It accelerates self-knowledge. Self-knowledge helps you make better decisions about your life and getting what you *really* want.)

Personality Qualities that Impact The "Me" Formula

Being accommodating & agreeable – there are some personality types that are more naturally accommodating than others because of their underlying *need to connect* with others as well as the need to please. These can be independent drivers or both can be at work at the same time.

How is that displayed? They are more likely to say yes to requests and then regret it later. Or, say yes to tasks and activities when there may not be available time to take it on. Or, say yes to things they genuinely don't want to do. These all can translate into over committing.

Natural decision-making styles – there are 4 natural decision-making styles: decisive, spontaneous, inclusive, and methodical (each with their own time management pros and cons).

Since this is one of the key components in the **Me Formula**, let's take a closer look.

Spontaneous: This type of decision-making is considered shooting from the hip or responding quickly with little fore thought. It is more emotion based than logic based.

In the case of spontaneous decision-making, saying yes can come quickly without a true sense of what's realistic and possible. This style is a common partner to being agreeable and accommodating. Sometimes spontaneous decision-makers feel stuck and stressed or even resentful, because they've said yes…now what?

Inclusive: Inclusive decision-makers like to have everyone participate in the decision making process. Some call it consensus building. This also might be a guise for feeling unsure or insecure in making a decision and so it's offered up to the group rather than taking the lead. For some inclusive decision-makers a desire to please can also be a subtle driver.

Decisive: Decisive decision-making is pretty cut and dry and suggests the decision is firm and unwavering. It's usually made quickly, and then you just go with it. Decisiveness exudes a sense of confidence even if the decision is made with limited information.

Methodical: Methodical decision-making implies making a decision in a step-by-step process; like considering one element at a time to build a case toward or away from a certain direction.

Methodical decision-makers can get very bogged down in this process however, and take too long to analyze all the elements. That's where the phrase "paralysis of analysis" comes in.

In referencing the **T-F-D-B formula**, you'll notice that decision-making is a key component. So one's natural decision-making style plays a major role in how this formula plays out.

Which style is the best one or right one? None of them! In fact, *effective decision-making is situational.* An important coaching tip – know you're natural style, but get good at all of them.

Please note - your natural style will play into how you apply what you'll learn in this book.

Also, I recommend you take the time to examine the pros & cons to all types as it relates to time management.

Left Brain or Right Brain – one of the main contributors to where you end up on a personality chart related to natural wiring is what thinking region of your brain has the most dominance; commonly known as the left brain or the right brain.

Though a bit over simplified, qualities of each are listed below. Consider:

- Where you fall the most
- How this impacts the Me Formula
- How it impacts the work and communication style while working in teams.

Left Brain –

Logical, reasoning, analytical, linear, black or white thinking, all or nothing, can't stand chaos, things have to fit, inflexible, task, and information orientated.

To the extreme: rigid, judgmental, rules rule, meticulous, over analytical

How does this play out in the context of this topic?

Examples:

-The left brain likes sequence (one thing at a time), so if there is a lot going on, left brainers may feel overwhelmed because their brain can't seem to break it down into manageable steps.

-Typically able to be and stay more focused for task completion and/or research.

-They can have tendencies towards perfectionism because for some left brainers there is a need to be right or correct.

-Additionally the left brain tends to be inflexible in it's thinking to the point where it's difficult to be open to new ideas or to switch gears quickly. It can get bogged down in too much planning, to the point of being excessive.

Right Brain –

Emotional, creative, open, mystical, intuitive, spontaneous, flexible, adaptive, people orientated.

To the extreme: may have difficulty coming to a single conclusion therefore making a decision, may infuse too much emotion into a situation and there by over complicate a situation, can be chaotic in thinking or expression of thoughts, difficulty being focused on task types of activities for long periods of time.

Examples:

-Natural idea generator or innovative thinking (outside the box).

-Able to adapt to changes with ease.

-Gets along well with just about anybody (accommodating).

-If you've ever heard of the phrase "multi-tasker" that's the right brain. If you're in a task driven environment right brainers tend to get bored easily, have a hard time bringing one task to completion before starting another and are easily distracted.

So in a task orientated work environment that would translate into this kind of work style: pick up, put down, start on something else, back to the other thing....you get the picture.

Right brainers also like working and connecting with people more than being isolated and working on tasks. They are the more naturally social members of a team.

Communication insight: right brainers tend to think and process out loud. To left brainers that might sound uninformed, disorganized, illogical or over explaining rather than getting to the point and that just drives them nuts!

The right brain / left brain dynamic impacts every area of your life: relationships, how you communicate with others, best job fit, natural work-style, and based on the Me Formula how you interpret and experience life.

All the examples for each brain directly impact the areas of focus in this book, both positively and negatively. It also impacts how time is spent as well as a team's interaction and productivity.

In what ways? *Here are a few examples:*

> ...who the natural interrupters might be
>
> ...who likes working alone
>
> ...how detailed a person's work product is or not

…who is able to build better rapport in a customer service or sales environment

We'll explore these and more throughout the book.

Take Time for Self-Assessment

So, where do you fit in the left brain/right brain descriptions? There are some people who are 50/50 right brain and left, but for most one is more dominate than the other.

How does that impact how you approach your work, work with others, and handle relationships?

I've left a space here for you to jot down some initial thoughts or any ah has you've had reading this section…take your time.

Additionally, if you're a manager (with a title) in any capacity – assess your team as well. The information you garner from your assessment can substantially impact how you manage.

 Notes

2. Life Conditioning

Consider this statement: You are the sum total of your conditioning to date. Another way of framing it - who you are is the composite of your life experiences.

Those life experiences have shaped (hard-wired) your thinking, behavior, beliefs, and values and serve as your current experience interpreter.

I would encourage you to consider how your life experience and upbringing has shaped your thinking to date.

Here is a list of the key sources of life conditioning. Take the time to contemplate these areas of influence and identify their impact in your adult life in ways that have been helpful and maybe not so helpful.

1. Family Conditioning (family culture, birth order, gender)

   Note: your family experiences are all recorded in your subconscious, which can be triggered at anytime.

   It also impacts brain development related to emotional intelligence.

2. Social Conditioning

   neighborhood where you grew up

   hobbies

   gender

schools you attended

spirituality

cultural

regional

country

generation

3. Work Experience Conditioning

industry

job types

length of time at company or job

company culture

relationship and types of supervisors and bosses

4. Emotional Intelligence or E.Q. (your ability to manage your emotions appropriately to any given situation).

All of those sources and how you've experienced them have shaped who you are, how you think, what you believe, and what you value.

Here is a shaping example from my own life related to hobby of sports. Growing-up I was very much involved in sports and leadership development thanks to attending a local Y.M.C.A. That experience allowed me to develop specific skills and level of confidence, which gave me the opportunity to play college volleyball without having played on a high-school team. I was even captain of the team my junior year!

Additionally, studies have reflected that girls involved in sports tend to have a higher self-esteem than those who don't.

Those experiences definitely impacted my personal development and how I functioned as I moved into my professional life after college.

3. Values

Values are defined as what matters most to you. People make decisions based on what they want and what's important to them.

A common situation in which values can be in conflict in many workplaces today is when multiple generations work together. The experience of what era you grew up in definitely shapes values and conditioning, which influences the "Me Formula."

As an example, let's use the context of management. As I travel across the country conducting management seminars, many times I hear the following:

Generation: Baby Boomers & Matures

"I have such a hard time managing Gen Xs and Gen Ys because they just don't seem to have a good work ethic."

Generation: Gen Xs and Gen Ys

"I have such a hard time managing Matures and Baby Boomers because they seem resistant to change and embracing new technology."

I'm sharing these statements not because I think they are true, but as an example of how this thinking can impact work experience interpretation.

The book *Generation X* summarizes these sentiments in this way, "Baby Boomers live to work - Gen Xs work to live."

So perhaps Gen Xs make different decisions than Baby Boomers do regarding the role work plays in their lives.

In the context of communicating, I've heard many Matures say they would rather just pick up the phone and call someone, where Gen Ys say they'd rather email or text.

Generational differences are an example of how values (what really matters) and pre-conditioning (via generation) shapes a philosophy or approach to work that then serves to influence decision making...should I stay late or not?....should I take work home or not....should I work on the weekend ....or not.

4. Beliefs

What's a belief? It's defined as follows:

: a state or habit of mind in which trust or confidence is placed in some person or thing:

: conviction of the truth of some statement or the reality of some being or phenomenon especially when based on examination of evidence

In thinking of the **Me Formula**, here is a practical example of what role beliefs would play in creating thoughts that generate feelings that lead to a certain kind of decision – reading a job description.

Let's say that you are looking at a job description and in reading that job description, your thought process goes like this… "Yeah, I think I can do that part. Yeah I definitely can do that… not sure if I can do that yet, but I'd like to learn to do that. Yes, I can do that too. That part sounds easy."

That thought process generates certain kinds of feelings. If you were to make a list of those feelings, you'd come up with encouraged, excited, confident…to name a few.

All those feelings are fueling motivation that would probably result in a decision that would generate the behavior or physical result of applying for the job.

Conversely, another person in his/her thought process might think like this: "I don't know for sure if I can do that. Well, I don't want to do that much work. Yeah, I can do that. I'm not going to do that either…hum, can't do that…don't want to do that.

These thoughts are generating negative feelings of discouragement and apathy that perhaps leads to disappointment, a lack of confidence, and even sadness.

Those emotions are de-motivating, which would probably result in the decision to not apply for he job.

So, there you can see from a very practical life example how the T F D B formula (Me Formula) plays out.

Give special note to the fact that emotions either motivate or de-motivate and the intensity of the emotion will determine the degree of motivation.

A Life Success Sidebar Regarding Beliefs

In considering the example of beliefs, it's important to recognize the following:

Just because someone tells himself or herself they can't do the job, doesn't mean they really can't do the job. It just means they don't believe they can.

Beliefs don't have to be true, real or rational. Whether true or not, they are a direct influence on how you experience life, the opportunities you do or do not take, or how you treat or react to someone.

I bet for many people, including myself, that opportunities have come your way but the beliefs did not support taking the opportunity.

Beliefs can be limiting, sabotaging, or empowering. I recommend you build an awareness of the beliefs you carry in your life in general and in each situation.

Remember, they are primarily automatic and subconsciously embedded. You'll need to take yourself off automatic to become fully aware.

Do you believe your emotional life is a time management-productivity issue?

Emotions & Decision Making

The Core of the T-F-D-B Formula

The core of this formula as it relates to the topic of time and organizational management is the **F => D (feelings drive & influence decision-making).**

In fact, every time management or how to get organized book should really be renamed "how to be an effective decision maker!"

Here is where the question comes in again, "how skilled am I at managing myself?"

When you look at the "me formula" you'll notice that one component of skilled decision-making lies in *effectively managing the emotions that influence and drive the decision.*

 The bottom line?... it's all about decision-making.

Every tip you'll find in any book on this topic

has to be executed with a decision.

Examples of Emotions in Decision Making

- *sentiment* or sense of nostalgia influences whether you keep things in your home or throw them away. It also impacts the reaction of workers who've worked at the same company for many years when changes are being made. Ever heard of the phrase, "but we've always done it that way?"

- *grief* surrounding the loss of a spouse influences the ability to move things out of a living space.

- and of course the all too familiar, classic statement of why papers are not thrown away in an office environment, "because I might need it some day," can be reframed to say, "I'm not throwing it away, because I'm afraid that if I might need it, I won't have it. The influencing emotion?...*fear!*

- also consider *pleasure*. I believe one of the main reasons why people procrastinate is because they do not find pleasure in the task at hand.

Fear is a big one. So let's park here for a moment and examine another scenario:

Scenario: At work - saying yes when you really want to say no to a request

Emotion: Fear

Fear of...you fill it in with your own words...

Being fired

Not being liked

Hurting someone's feelings

Not being seen as a team player

Causing someone to become angry

Failure

Disappointing someone

Of the unknown

Not getting a raise

It's clear that emotions drive and influence decision-making. And for those of you who might consider yourselves logical decision makers, recent studies of the brain indicate that even in the context of a logical decision, the emotional parts of the brain still light up.

Here's an essential question that must be answered before you move on.

How aware are you of what emotions influence or drive your decision-making and in what situation or context?

I recommend that you do a **30 day emotion audit** tracking your emotions and looking for patterns and trends. You can simply do so by having a piece of paper at your desk and tuning in when you're making a decision, become conscious of what or who is involved recording the date and time.

The goal of the audit is to build awareness around the emotions you use to make decisions and to see if that's what you consciously want. Ask yourself, "what's working for me and what's not?" Then make a plan to manage it differently.

Example: When I'm making a decision while using online travel services, I became aware that I was spending too much time examining options, sometimes wrestling over a difference of just a few dollars. I have in this case challenged myself to make decisions faster. I literally say in my head, "Speed it up."

Stop & Consider

This is a very important point to capture before you move forward so to follow is a brief exercise. I've left an area blank for you to write your thoughts.

✐ Gage your current awareness of *emotions that influence and drive decision-making – note examples from your life and add other emotions to the list.*

Anger

Pleasure

Frustration

Joy

Love

Sense of competition

Desire for achievement

Overwhelmed

Guilt

Greed

Fear

Need for something to be perfect

Life Success Side-Bar

Managing Emotions and Health

One additional reason why this is an important and worthwhile exercise is related to the issue of health.

Ever heard of the phrase," toxic feelings" or even "toxic people?" The term toxic references the fact that certain emotions release distinct kinds of chemicals in the brain that in large doses over an extended period of time can lead to ill health.

For example: Have you ever been around a person who is so habitually negative that you feel that the life is being sucked right out of you? In that situation, feelings of low energy and even exhaustion are a result of certain chemicals being released from the brain during that encounter. One well-publicized chemical is the stress hormone Cortisol.

Here's the key – elevated levels of Cortisol in the body over an extended period of time can actually lead to disease and the activation of other illnesses. It can even influence something as simple as the activation of fat receptors in the body causing excess belly fat.

So another important reason for the audit?...track how your decision-making is impacting your health either in a positive or negative way.

The Bottom Line...

It's all about decisions that generate behaviors
that create habits.

Consider this formula: consistent behaviors = habits = results

In fact, did you know that the sum total of your life could be spelled out with five letters? That's right - **H A B I T**. **Habits are automated behaviors. They produce consistent, automated results.**

We each have automated behaviors that get the desired results and the undesired results in life. Ultimately in changing anything in your life, it's helpful to view it through the lens of habits.

With that in mind, building an awareness of your habits is the final component needed as you begin your journey to improve the "Me in Team and Time." Building awareness means taking yourself off automatic pilot and becoming more conscious of what you're doing.

Here's a quick exercise:

Identify a positive, consistent behavior in your life by filling in the blank below:

I'm in the habit

of_____

Now identify something you'd like to change, but identifying it as a habit…fill in the blank again.

I want to develop the habit

of_____

Habits are the hard-wired behaviors created and mapped in your brain, sourced primarily from your subconscious. The hard wiring, simply put, is the neural pathways mapped through doing or thinking the same things over and over again.

So in order for a change to occur or a new habit to be created, a new neural pathway has to be built. **The key – the new action has to happen consistently and long enough for the new pathway to be built while not providing an opportunity for the old pathway to continue being used.**

This is one reason people get discouraged when setting and then not meeting their New Year's Resolution or other behavior based goals. The attempt to change does not happen long enough for the neural pathway to be created.

I'd like to close this section with a poem devoted to the word habit.

HABIT

"I am your constant companion; I am your greatest helper or your heaviest burden. I will push you onward or drag you down to failure. I'm completely at your command.

Half the things you do you might just as well turn over to me and I will be able to do them quickly and correctly. I am easily managed. You must merely be firm with me.

Show me exactly how you want something done and after a few lessons I will do it automatically. I am the servant of all great men and the ally of all failures as well. Those who are great, I have made great. Those who are failures, I have made failures.

I am not a machine although I work with all the precision of a machine plus the intelligence of a man. You may run me for profit or run me for ruin. It makes no difference to me. Take me, train me, be firm with me and I'll put the world at your feet. Be easy with me and I will destroy you. Who am I? I am HABIT!"

Section 2

Managing Your

Space & Stuff

"Less IS more."

Managing Your Space & Stuff

It's All About "Find-ability & Scan-ability"

We're now going to take the ME in time formula and apply it to the practical – how to part of the book.

As a reminder, the point of this section is not to be organized for the sake of being organized, but to improve efficiency so that you can produce more and better results; essentially getting the right things done at the right time.

In my workshops across the country, I have found that people are inundated with stuff that comes into their workspace and feel as if it's just gotten out of control.

So let's get started. As you consider the TFDB formula (Me Formula), shift your thinking to some of the basic things you do in your workspace.

> **Power point:**
>
> Your goal in this section of managing space and stuff is to **have space and a work surface**.

The first thing to consider is this: (and I know this sounds grossly oversimplified, but it's for a reason) your workspace is really to *execute work*. Just putting that out there for you.

Your workspace is to have *space to work*. And in order to do that more effectively with less stress, you need a *work surface*. I know that sounds crazy, but if you really look at it that way, your goal is to **have space and a surface**. Your two keywords?…**space and surface.**

Want Space?

Principles for Arranging Your Space

> *"You cannot solve a problem*
> *at the same level of thinking at which you arrived at it."*
>
> *-Albert Einstein*

If you work at all in a cluttered workspace or just want to rearrange it, you need to start by re-imagining it. Referencing Albert Einstein's quote above, when we work in the same space or with the same material, we get bogged down in the familiar and that makes is more difficult to see it differently or take a fresh approach.

Let's re-imagine your space for a second and have this thought process: I want to have the best space I can to execute work, to have the most *work surface* to execute work with the least amount of stress.

Additionally, I want my work area to be scan-able. I want to be able to scan and locate something within a reasonable period of time with the least amount of stress to myself or someone else (e.g. colleague or family member).

With that in mind, here are some key principles that you'll want to consider that will help you create that re-imagined space.

As a reminder, when considering these principles it's all about finding and gaining your 1%.

Principle #1 - Think Zones

The first principle to consider is to see your work area in zones. Your work area has primarily 3 zones: A, B, and C. Looking at the diagram below, you'll notice there is an X. That's you sitting at the place you

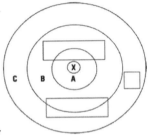

spend the majority of time when you're executing work and that's called the Arc space. Sit at your work surface and place your elbow in the middle. Keeping your elbow still, move your arm right to left – that is your ARC space.

The Arc space is part of your "A" space. In zoning, the "A" space is not only where you work the most, but should also house things that you need to reach immediately or within a cycle of a day.

The B-space then, should house things that you use within a cycle of a week.

The C-space should house things you need access to within a cycle of one to two months. And with that, try not to use your work area for storage.

A quick disclaimer before I go on: I know that there are a variety of people reading this book with varied job descriptions coming from a lot of different industries. With that in mind, you'll need to customize these principles based on your unique circumstances.

So consider these principles not as rules but guidelines. I'm about guidelines that get results. (Remember our phrase from earlier – rules should not rule us.) *If you've got something that's working for you, keep doing it!*

Principle #2 - Think Energy

Consider this - inanimate objects have energy. What does that mean to you? Too many things – clutter for example - is like a force.

A desk is hard matter, yet is comprised of moving protons, neutrons, atoms, etc. Even though it's inanimate (hard and not moving to the naked eye – not a living organism) it's got energy to it.

How do you know that? Have you ever been in a cluttered space, cleaned it out and then did this, (breath) and said to yourself, "Now I can breathe."

Consider this: when you are in a workspace that has a lot of stuff, it takes more physical energy to work in it. All of those things in your workspace are sucking up energy and oxygen and you physically have to work harder just to think and execute work. You could go home exhausted not only from the work, but the space in which the work is done.

Principle # 3 - Less is More

The less you have in your workspace, the more energy and air you have to execute work with more ease and less mental and physical stress. You can experience a sense of more efficiency.

Principle #4 - Visual Noise

Another example of visual noise is the **e-mail indicator**.

Recommendation: If you are not e-mail driven at your organization, turn off the indicator and schedule checking your e-mail instead.

This leads to the 4th principle and that is **Visual Noise**. What does that mean to you? It can be translated as clutter and/or interference; particularly if you have difficulty focusing. When you have a lot of things around, it calls for your attention and can be a mental disruption.

As you work with these principles, you'll notice your ability to think more clearly, execute work with more energy, and reduce physical and mental stress.

How will you rearrange your work area?

✐Notes

5 Power Practices to Maintain Your Space

Now that you've looked at how to arrange your space for more efficiency, you'll need to keep your work area and work surface as clear as possible on an on-going basis.

To follow are **5 Practices** you'll want to incorporate as regular work habits. And as a reminder, consider these as competencies in the context of getting results.

Also, all five of these when applied, can help you achieve your 1% in any situation; whether it's your garage, your house, your bedroom, or your online activity.

As your read through these five practices, think of each in the context of these questions: should it be a habit?... should it be a lifestyle?

Practice #1:   Sort – quickly & regularly

What is sorting? Simply put, deciding what to do with something, categorizing...

...what to keep, what to through away...and it's all about the D's. What's the D word? It's all about decision-making. Ah, here it is ...T-F-D-B...what you think and how you feel will dictate how you sort.

Here again is where this question plays a critical role, "How skilled am I at managing myself…my thinking…my feelings?"

Self-management and the TFDB piece plays an essential role here. I think you'll begin to see more and more that managing yourself in a variety of contexts is really the critical component to this entire book!

Please note that being more skilled at sorting is housed in the knowledge that sorting tends to bog people down. I believe it's because too much is trying to be accomplished in one action.

Here's where the concept of micro-steps comes in, that is breaking down actions into mini-steps. **So consider sorting as a singular, complete action.** That way working through a pile or group of anything won't create overwhelm.

Practice #2: Purge

Next, you've got to be able to do this on a regular basis - purge. (You know how words sound like what they are? Doesn't purge sound like purge? It's kind of like stuff sounds like stuff).

What is purging?…getting rid of. Should purging be a lifestyle? Should it be a habit? Yes. That could be your 1% right there. Ask yourself or even make a list of what needs to be purged right now, both off line and on line?

In purging, let's consider the T-F-D-B formula. As you're thinking about what to keep or what to throw away, be aware of any emotions and their varying degrees and how that is influencing your decision-making.

Practice #3: Assign

The next practice to maintain space and surface is to assign. Assign means make a decision about where to put it.

The overriding principle is, **"everything must have a home."** The theory is – if it has a home, it's easier and more likely that it will be put back. Do you have things in your office, home or garage that are homeless? Do you have a few floaters that don't have a permanent home?

For sure you have things on your work surface that you know for a fact are at home; for example, your stapler. That's a common tool. I guarantee you if one of your colleagues "borrowed" your stapler, you would know it! Why?...because that stapler has a home.

So the home can be a slot on your desk or a designated spot on your bookshelf. It could be a lot of different things. But the premise is - if it has a home, you're more likely *and able* to put it back, which serves to help you maintain your space and keep your work surface cleared. How many times have you said, "I don't know where to put this." The result?...it's laid somewhere and that begins a stack or pile.

Here's where you entertain the possibility that you might have too much stuff. You may need to ask yourself, "Should I or can I create a home for this item?"

It might be a slot on a shelf, a slot on your desk, or, it could be an item under practice #4.

Breaking it down is called making a

"micro-decision."

Practice #4:   Contain

A home could be a container. You know what? I love that word. Take it in the most literal sense - what does it do? Contain. If stuff, paper, etc. is contained, it can't escape. It can't grow. It can't procreate.

Ever heard of the laws of stuff? One of the key laws - stuff grows. You just put a little stuff down, and all of a sudden what happens to that pile? It has fiestas, asks the neighbors over and before you know it, that one little pile of stuff has turned into a big pile of stuff!

Now, if it is contained, it can't grow or escape. So you've got to *contain* it. Just containing can give you your 1%. Just containing can give you more work surface and more workspace.

Additionally, consider two other "c" practices - **colorize and categorize**. In order to up your organizational factor, you'll be able to identify a container much more quickly if it's assigned a category and a color.

So the main point here is to segment and break it down. If you just sort and contain, there would be progress and would create immediate surface and space.

Can You Grab & Go?

In the spirit of the title of this book, I'm going to give you a challenge (since I'm your self-appointed coach at least for the duration of this book). Here it is – **The One Minute Grab &Go.**

There are two parts to **The 1 Minute Grab & Go Challenge**:

1. Can you go into your work area and find something within one minute for the Grab and Go?
2. Can you direct a colleague from a phone to go into your work area and find something for the Grab and Go? These are the two conditions for **The 1 Minute Grab & Go Challenge.**

Now some of you are probably thinking, I got that part down. Some are thinking … one minute? You've got to be kidding me!

 For the doubters who don't think this is a fair challenge, here's what I'd like for you to do. I want you to let one minute elapse getting a sense or gauge of 1 minute. Test if it's a fair challenge. Starting now, you're going to let one minute elapse.

That was one minute. Now you know the adage if you're watching time it goes by slower. However, if you felt like it was about one minute and that was about normal for you, then that's great. If you felt like it felt like forever or more than a minute you may be experiencing a bit of time distortion.

What's time distortion? Time distortion is not having a realistic sense of time. In a lot of busy organizations employees work out of time distortion; decisions are made in time distortion. Now imagine - you're already in time distortion and then decisions are made in distortion...what's that going to do? I say...increase stress.

So where does the time distortion piece come from? Salt Lake City, Utah did a 911 study and in doing so asked this question -- how long did it take the emergency response vehicle to arrive? The answers reflected that the more intense the trauma, the longer it felt for the ambulance to arrive.

For example, a lady's husband had a heart attack and her answer to the question was "at least ten minutes." How long did the log say?...five.

This is an interesting prelude to the time management section. It's my deepest belief that many function so much in distortion at work, that very unrealistic expectations are set for work and that's what causes so much stress.

We'll expound upon this further in the time management section. But let me make this point now... **In general, (both at work and at home) most people have no idea how long things take to do.**

Ok – let's go back to The 1 Minute Grab & Go Challenge. Do you think the one minute challenge for the grab and go is realistic? I encourage you to take that challenge.

Take a **Virtual Field Trip** at an online office supply site to explore all the containing possibilities.

Also, think of how to repurpose items (use for their not intended use).

For example: when I travel I use a small glasses case to hold my pens, so I can easily find them when on the go.

The best way to be consistently successful at this challenge is to make sure the 3 "Cs" are in use.

So here is your guideline – if it is not **containerized, colorized, or categorized** enough, then you will not effectively be able to do the grab and go.

Now, let's park on the container piece for a moment. I'd also like for you to re-imagine that. Name (or make a list of) some containers, and I invite you to be creative. *Here are a few suggestions to get you started:*

A box, a file folder, a drawer, a cupboard, bookshelf, plastic tubs, car glove box, truck, glasses case, envelope, file pocket, hanging folder, file cabinet, hard drive, zip lock bag, pencil case, magazine holder, and document sleeves.

Now here is where we get creative and take the word "contain" to its literal meaning: a rubber band, a binder clip, a staple, paper clip. All of these items *contain*.

Practice #5: Equalize

The last of the five practices is to equalize. Got any idea what that means? It means to put things back in their homes. A simple example is parents asking their kids to put their toys back – that's equalizing.

Here's another example and suggestion on how to incorporate equalizing: Let's say your goal is to **keep your A space clear**. Let's also say you have had just a heck of a day. You've got stuff strewn everywhere. Stop and take the time to do what? Just clean out your A-space - equalize it; that way you just don't pile disorder on top of more disorder. **Equalizing should be a regular ritual – whether daily or weekly (both online and off line).**

Here's the thing – you'll have difficulty finding things if they're not containerized, colorized, or categorized enough. These very simple principles can go a long way.

Equalizing also really helps with the grab & go.

Summary & Action Plan

Ok, we've made it through the 5 practices of having and maintaining your surface and space. If you take the first letter of each tip, it becomes an acronym for the word **SPACE.**

Sort   **P**urge   **A**ssign   **C**ontain   **E**qualize

Here is the cool part. It's not only 5 practices but serves as a system as well. It's a practical system on how to maintain space. It honors the definition of organize, "systematic planning."

Also, it's easy to remember and it applies to any situation both online and off.

WORKSHEET PAGE

Stop - Consider - Make a Plan - Take Action

Here is where you want to stop, regroup, and consider what you want to apply first. I encourage you to try something…apply something daily for at least 7-14 days. Please note that it is not my expectation that you go through this book all at once, but use it as an ongoing guide or portable coach.

Additionally, a self-coaching tip you may want to employ is using the reoccurring feature on your calendar or a post-it note for a daily reminder prompt toward any action you want to practice.

Coaching Questions:

Have you found your 1% from any one of these?

Which one of these do you want to practice and get really good at?

How will you use your calendar reoccurring feature or sticky note to coach yourself?

I want to become skilled at _____.

From your reading so far, what's stuck?

As a manager, how or what do I want to incorporate with my team collectively or individually?

Section 3

Managing Information

Where is all the knowledge we lost with information?

T.S. Elliot

Managing Information

Who's the person that said that computers would generate less paper? Remember when only "snail mail" existed? Ok...for some readers maybe not.

If you're like those in my seminars, there is a steady stream of paper, information, and stuff in a variety of forms that congregate in work areas and sometimes just feels as if it's all taking over.

In the 21st century work environment, **managing information is a new professional competency**. Being skilled at managing information will dictate how much time you'll have to actually execute work and here is where gaining your 1% can really make a difference.

I define managing information in a very simple, practical way – can I find what I'm looking for with minimal stress? To be able to do that, you'll need to continue to re-imagine your workspace. Now see it as scan-able. Can I scan my space so I can find what I am looking for?

So let's go back and be reminded of our opening section and the definition "to manage."

Define: to handle and direct with some degree of skill

As it relates to this section consider this question: <u>How skilled am I at handling and directing what enters my work area?</u> How skilled am I at finding something quickly?

In order to answer that question and to get a handle on your "handling"….here is an additional question that is critical to answer:

Do you know your information flow?

When you read that question, what does it mean to you?

In essence, you have information and items flowing into your work area all the time, both tangible and virtual. **In order to handle it effectively, you need to know what's coming into your work area and what you're doing with it.**

For the moment, I'd like for you to think off line and then you'll apply it to online later.

To answer that question, here is what you'll need to do: *create an information flow chart.* List all of the things that come into your office and then track-indicate what you do with them. In some cases your list will indicate that you put some in piles or a stackable tray, trash container or file folder.

The purpose of the **Flow Chart** is to build awareness of the behaviors that in many cases are done unconsciously – the habits you've developed in handling the flow of information coming into your space.

And also to employ the principle, "everything must have a home." *Each item on your information flow chart should have a purposed home.*

To follow are items that may appear on your **Information Flow Chart** and where you might be placing them:

Snail mail – *stackable tray (in box)*

Fed Ex

Self- generated documents – *file folders categorized*

faxes – *in box*

invoices – *stackable tray*

meeting notes – *spiral notebook*

printed e-mails – *categorized folder*

expense reports

interoffice documents

voicemail messages

Reminder: We're working with these principles...

Find-ability

Grab & Go

Is my office scan-able?

Of course your list will look a bit different. Again, the purpose of this exercise is to take yourself off automatic pilot and build an awareness around how you habitually handle items that come into your workspace, to consciously determine a home for them, and to determine what is working for you and what is not.

If you're finding yourself surrounded by piles, with stacks on the floor, and unable to locate items for *The Grab & Go*, consider the recommendations to follow to maintain your work surface and space.

Also, as you consider the principles to follow, keep in mind the earlier question: can I scan my work area so that I can find it?

Let's start off with these paper management truths:

- √ Flat creates a stack.
- √ If it's not contained, it will grow.
- √ When documents and files are lying flat, they are harder to see or locate quickly.

Recommendations: Keep & Work Vertically

Flat creates a stack - vertical I can see for the grab and go.

So what does that mean exactly? Instead of laying files flat - keep them standing up. You can find very inexpensive office supplies like plastic vertical stands that are all one level or tiered. Examples:

You can also use accordion folders or file jackets because they can stand on their own. Additionally they come in different colors, and expand to different sizes.

Expanded file pockets also come in handy when you're working on a project that requires multiple file folders. You can grab the whole accordion folder for the grab and go.

Sort Vertical: Instead of sorting into piles, sort directly in files. For example, take the items out of your *in basket* or in tray. Now start sorting into folders. This is a new habit or pattern of behavior - a new way of *handling and directing*.

The simple goal is to go from sorting into flat stacks or piles to sorting into vertical folders.

Since sorting into stacks for some is such an embedded habit, it really will take some time to permanently create a new automated way of managing documents & folders. I suggest giving yourself at least 45 days of focused effort to turn this into a new habit.

Use a Customized Filing System for <u>Your</u> Work

Here's what I mean. Usually a company has its own filing system. Yet, when it comes to your work domain, I recommend you create your own unique filing system that helps you find things quickly.

Honestly, no one can really tell you what filing system you should use within your own domain. If you're going to find something, it must be based on *how you think* – so you can find it. That's why the flow chart is an important tool and exercise – it lays out how you think.

Make a List of Themes & Categories You Encounter

With that in mind, go to your flow chart and take a moment to identify core categories that you work with and assign those categories a color. Use this as your source for going from piles into files.

Remember - files (folders) are containers, they are homes, they keep things from turning into stacks and make it easier to locate something when you need to do the "grab & go."

Have Working Folders & Temporary Holding Folders

How you use folders is key to scanning your work area so you can find something quickly. I recommend using two categories in your customized filing plan while adopting this mantra:

Files are not necessarily for filing – they are for finding.

The two categories are Working Folders & Temporary Holding Folders.

Working Folders – are those that are part of your own filing system. They are the folders that are considered *active*, housing information you'll need access to on a regular basis.

I recommend that they be colored. However, if you don't wish to purchase colored folders or are on the low, low, low budget, take bright fluorescent highlighters and color the tabs of manila folders.

Temporary Holding Folders - As you're working through your papers, have something called temporary holding folders. These folders can house documents that you may not know what to do with or you know don't belong in a Working Folder or may need to be matched with additional information. There are lots of uses for this concept. You'll have to decide how best to use this folder idea. The point is - it's a home so it doesn't turn into a pile.

For labeling, you can also use a pencil or a colored sticky note. When I get a document that doesn't have an obvious home, I write on the manila tab and it goes in the vertical folders arranged by alphabet.

Once a decision about a document has been made, I then erase the tab and use the folder again. When I spot check (scan) my vertical files, any that are manila means it's temporary.

Additionally you will want to have categories and containers for storing or archiving as well.

> Sorting vertically is considered a *micro-step*.
>
> The point of it is to prevent piles.
>
> It's simply containing so the pile can't grow.

In summary being able to find something is based on where you put it. To find it, it must have a home.

Your goal is to find something with the least amount of stress. Period. How can I find it for the grab and go?

When you're creating your information flow chart, remember the 3 C's of find-ability, scan-ability, and the grab & go -- *containerize, colorize or categorize.*

By the way, these days there are lots of cool tools to use to colorize besides folders. Again, take a virtual or real field trip to your local office supply store and look at items through the lens of the principles you've read so far. Determine how you can increase your find-ability and scan-ability factor.

Examples: binder clips, staples, post-it notes, document sleeves, and rubber bands. All of these come in a variety of styles, sizes and colors.

The Power of Color

The ultimate of the 3 C's is color. Even if something is lying flat, if it's tagged or contained with a bright color it will be easier to spot.

And if you don't want to go vertical, you can stair step your stacks and contain with a binder clip or label with a brightly colored post it note. Remember, it's all about find-ability and scan-ability incorporating the 3 C's – containerize, colorize, and/or categorize.

One of my favorite containers is a magazine holder. Do you have magazines...get periodicals, brochures, catalogs? Those items may have shown up on your *Information Flow Chart.* Magazine holders are great containers and come in multiple sizes and styles.

The best way to use one is to use the smallest size (width) available.

When I was working to de-clutter my office I was working with a volume of magazine subscriptions. I challenged myself to reduce the amount of magazine stacks and subscriptions.

So I got a holder for each subscription (the smallest one) and used the principle of once this is full, when I get a new issue, I will take out the oldest edition.

Here's what I discovered -- how little I was actually reading the magazines. That was an ah-ha moment! I challenged myself to only subscribe to the few I did read, and then scheduled time to go to the library to read others. I did cancel many subscriptions. The result?...I saved money, got more reading done, and reduced the piles and clutter in my office!

Reducing or Eliminating Piles

If your piles are working for you, meaning you or someone else can find something with minimal effort, then keep working in that way. If they're not working for you though, then you may want to consider going completely vertical.

Additionally, if you have piles that you want to reduce or eliminate, here's a tip to do so without overwhelming yourself - its' call **The Three Dot Method** for reducing piles.

The Three Dot Method for Reducing Piles

This is a wonderful technique for getting rid of piles and developing the skill of quick decision-making, and it leverages the power of your subconscious mind.

I really believe that the success of sorting through paper is that you not only make it fun, but also only do it for short bursts of time.

The first step in the **Three Dot Method** is to choose 3 minutes in a time of the day that is consider your "down time", meaning low energy vs. a peak period time.

Next choose 3 days within a week that you will do it. It doesn't matter which ones.

Next, block out that time and place as a recurring feature in your electronic calendar. If you don't have one, place a post-it-note where it can be regularly viewed.

Now, let's say you have several piles of paper you'd like to sort through. Take the first stack and place it in front of you with a colored pen of your choice and a trash container at your side. If you're going to go vertical, have your file folders set up (both Working Folders & manila folders for your Temporary Holding Folders).

As you start going through your papers, the key is to **sort quickly** – don't belabor or over analyze the documents. For some documents, you won't be able to make an immediate decision. When you get to a document that you don't know what to do with, take your colored pen, put a dot on the bottom corner, left or right depending on what hand you use, and *quickly put it underneath your pile.* DO NOT start another pile! Don't judge it, don't beat yourself up about it, and don't belabor the decision. **Your goal is to go through the stack fast!**

Continue to go through the rest of stack #1- some of the documents will be filed, some will be thrown away and a few will be left. The remaining documents will have 1 dot on them. Take what's left of that pile and put it on top of the next one. You now have one pile done – yeah!

The next time it comes up in your recurring feature, grab that next pile. Now in this pile you'll have some with no dots and some with 1 dot.

All right, you're now going through the next pile and, oh, there's a document with one dot and you still don't know what to do with it – that's okay. Don't judge it - don't belabor it. Just put a dot on it and put it where?...*on the bottom*. **The goal is to get through the pile. How fast? Quickly.**

Now you may have some in that pile that have one dot and you may have some that have two dots. Take the finished pile, whatever is left over, and place it on the next pile. So how many piles have you gotten done? Two!

You'll go next to pile three when it pops up on your calendar. This time you'll have some with no dots, some with one, and some with two. Go through the same procedure as before.

Trust me on this – once you get to pile three, you're going to start making decisions faster. Somehow in your brain it starts to train you to be more decisive.

As you continue going through the piles, you're going to come to some documents with two dots on them. You can put a third - that's fine. Continue to sort quickly putting it on the bottom – do not stall the process by over analyzing the document. Just feel the excitement of making it through the pile as fast as you possibly can. When you get done with that pile, whatever's left, put it on top of the next pile.

When you get to the papers that have three dots on them, here is what's likely to happen. Number one - you will throw it away. Number two – this is the coolest part about how the brain works – your subconscious will have seen it enough to actually help you decide. This is employing a fun practice also used in creative thinking.

When your subconscious sees something over and over again and you ask it a question…it will go to work to answer the question for you! The same thing with decision-making, once you sleep on something and you see it several times, the decision becomes clear. That's where the phrase, "let me sleep on it" comes from.

When you review a document it's being recorded in your subconscious mind. The more your subconscious sees it, the more it starts to develop an opinion about it and the decision-making becomes effortless.

So the self-coaching principle for managing and eventually getting rid of your piles is called **The Three Dot Rule.**

A Final Note About Piles & Dots

Honestly, at some point you'll just get tired of seeing dots and you'll say to yourself, "Okay, this is ridiculous, I've got to get rid of these dots." This will prompt you to become more decisive. And as a final step, should you have any dotted documents left, you can place them in a temporary holding folder labeled, "Three Dots".

Principle – All In One Place

Ok, that was such an involved explanation of getting rid of piles; let me remind you of what's being discussed. We're going through a list of recommendations on how to manage your information flow.

The next recommendation then is the principle of "all in one place." *Here is a context to view this principle:*

When you filled out your flow chart, what did you record concerning your meeting notes and telephone messages - where do you put them? Ever used multiple legal pads for notes?

The principle of *all in one place* is for notes, meetings, telephone messages, etc. It could be a spiral pad. It could be a binder and loose leaf paper. It could be a file pocket or a digital format.

The tool is not as important as the principle. I use to use multiple legal pads and then I had an incredibly stressful experience.

When I lived in Chicago I lived in the western suburbs and had clients downtown. I had a pretty big account I was working on landing and I had previous meeting notes on one of my many yellow legal pads.

I was in my office and I needed to pack quickly to get downtown. So I grabbed the notepad I thought those meeting notes were on, put it in my briefcase along with other materials and got to the Sears Tower comfortably on time.

I sat in the conference room, pulled out my notes, only to find it was the wrong notepad. Honestly, I still feel it now - my heart absolutely sank. So I had to conduct that meeting completely off the top of my head – talk about stress! Never again I thought and with that created something called the **1 Pad Challenge**.

Though 1 singular legal pad ended up not really working, I did go to a spiral notebook. I still had to categorize, even though it was all in one place.

Lately I've gone to a notebook with loose-leaf paper on a small portable clipboard. It still employs the same principle, just uses different tools.

So you may want to consider **the 1 pad challenge**. It's much easier to find something if it is in all in one place. I did have someone in my seminar that just loved legal pads and had certain pads designated for certain activities, but they were all one color. So I suggested she color-code the pads. She loved the idea!

This brings up another important point. Tools need to be fluid, because our needs are fluid. Both our personal and work lives are ever evolving and at times will require a reassessment of tools and practices to meet current needs. Have you found that just when you get it all down, something changes. Awhhh life – it has such a sense of humor!

Context: Telephone messages, conversations with co-workers or your boss when they walk into your workspace

Where do you put telephone messages?...notes from a conversation for reference or requires an action? Go back to your information flow – when you get telephone messages what do you do with them? Where do you record them? Where can you access them?

I like keeping a journal of activities every day. With loose-leaf paper, it's easy to put in a loose-leaf binder and find quickly – I just number the pages. A spiral notebook also meets this need really well. You can always go back and reference what you're looking for because it's *all in one place.*

Let's Take a Breather

I recommend at this point that you *start an action list* from what you've read so far. Then decide what you'll focus on first and just do that one thing until you see results.

As you continue to read and things come to your attention that you'd like to apply, write them down. You could end up with an action list that you could implement over the course of the next year.

Here's why I say the next year. If you focused on one thing a quarter-that is every 90 days, over the course of 1 year, look at the progress that can be made with this approach.

Consider how much more productive you would be over the course of that year.

That's the power of the 1%.

✑ Write Your Summary Notes

E-MAIL MANAGEMENT

Is it safe to say that in today's workplace we spend about as much time managing e-mail as getting actual work done? Too much e-mail in fact can feel like "electronic clutter." And because of that, many of the strategies and principles already discussed can be applied to e-mail as well.

I do believe this is another of the competencies I mentioned in the introduction that needs to be developed. *Effective email management is a skill.*

If you can manage your email 1% better - you'll create more time to get more work done. With the suggestions to follow, find your 1% edge.

Email can be an effective way of communicating, but I believe and have experienced, that the lack of skill in using it just creates more work. A lot of time is wasted with email.

So as we begin this section, I recommend you adopt this mindset:

Email is a tool to manage the virtual experience. It is a tool to work with people through a process to get to a result. (So is text and the phone for that mater).

You know there are a lot of expectations when people communicate virtually that are in their head but don't get put on paper.

Here's what I mean. How many times have you gotten a request for something from a colleague and there was no indication of when it's needed - no time and date? How many emails don't have enough information in them and therefore requires 3 or 4 more email exchanges just to get from point A to point B.

Because most people do not use email effectively, I recommend developing this skill:

Be more specific, informative, & directive when using and writing emails.

So what is specific, informative and directive? *Tell people what to think, how to behave, and what to expect* as specifically as possible.

For example - have a format or template that you use on a regular basis. If someone sends a request for something and it doesn't have all the information, send it back with specific instruction on exactly what you need at the exact time and date you need it.

In some cases you already to do this. When I'm conducting a seminar I ask, "How many of you have your out of office reply on?" Many raise their hand. Then I ask then to share what it says. Many will say, "I'll be out of the office on x day returning on x date. If you need assistance call x at extension 3560."

That is a great example of instructive, informative, and directive. It clearly illustrates **tell them what to think – what to expect – how to behave.**"

Coaching Tip:

Use Coaching Prompts

Whenever you're trying to develop a new habit, put a post-it note on your computer that has the behavior written out. In this case you'd want to have the words: instructive, directive and informative as a constant reminder.

Here's the overriding point to remember: e-mail like voicemail is a tool to manage a virtual experience and relationship in the context of trying to execute work. It's about managing behavior, results, *and* expectations.

It's useful to think: "I'm managing my relationship (or experience) with this person and I'm communicating with them through e-mail, and that's apart of a relationship. This person has a personality. This person has a work style with certain characteristics that are either helping me or hindering me and I need to communicate in a way to coach that person so that I get the results I want in the most efficient and effective way."

And here's a side note - in some cases the most efficient action you can take is to pickup the phone! I'm sure there are times when you could execute something quicker if you just picked up the phone. A five-minute conversation might be the better choice.

Of course there needs to be an effective use of the phone as well. I just think sometimes we forget about picking up the phone because we're so conditioned to use email.

The E-mail Overwhelms

Have you ever experienced e-mail overwhelm? I believe that the same thing happens with e-mail that happens with paper - when you try to do it all at once – sort, decide, and work on it, you might start to feel bogged down or overwhelmed.

Now I know that working with e-mail is personal and unique to each individual. For some, having a full inbox all the time doesn't faze them; yet for others, the site of a full inbox causes a cold sweat.

So as you consider working with your e-mail, perhaps the question to ask is, "What about my e-mail do I want to change?" What about how I currently handle email is not working for me?"

There are no hard and fast "shoulds." If something is working for you then don't change it.

But if something isn't, focus on applying a principle – or new behavior to it.

For example: To keep my e-mail count manageable, I've started purging once a day for 3 minutes. Quite frankly I'm amazed at what I can delete in that short period of time. (Actually, it's amazing how much you can do in 1 minute.)

Additionally, I have *changed my expectation* of the amount of e-mail in my inbox. I just regularly ask myself, "Am I effectively managing it and is it managing me or am I managing it?"

At this point it'd be helpful to ask yourself, "What have I learned so far that applies to better e-mail management?" What have I learned that are principles I can apply to gain my 1%?"

Answers so far:

- Purging for a minute. Purging as a habit. Purge daily. Keep going....
- Sorting – "sort quickly"
- Sort for a set period of time
- Working Folders – Temporary Holding Folders
- Even the S.P.A.C.E. acronym is a system of managing email

Let's expand on these and add a few more.

Summary Strategies & Ideas for Email

As you work through the principles to follow, I recommend you consider your e-mail in-box your *digital work surface.*

#1 – Sort Quickly

Don't allow yourself to get bogged down trying to do too many steps at once.

#2 – Use Temporary Holding Folders

In sorting quickly, sort into temporary holding folders. The key here is to train yourself **to make quick decisions** to get your e-mail moved to identifiable areas as quickly as possible.

In combining both of those tips, consider that when sorting your e-mail you only have 4 choices to make - **action – refer – reference - delete**. You could use a *temporary holding folder for the action e-mails* – to house them for the moment to get them out of your inbox.

You may need other temporary holding folders and how you label your temporary holding folders is up to you. Just remember to make it as simple as possible whatever you name them - it's all about finding.

#3 – Use the 3 "Cs" To Make Your

E-mail Scan-able

It saves a lot of time when you can locate emails quickly. The search feature also helps here.

The principles discussed earlier – containerize, colorize, and categorize also work very effectively with e-mail.

Organizing Email Folders

Most e-mail systems automatically alphabetize. There are other ways to supersede that to ensure the folders you really want on top appear there. Prior to the formal title of the folder, consider the following:

- Use letters with a dash
- Space before the title of the folder
- Use symbols such as (@, &, #, _, *) prior to title
- Use numbers

As a reminder, the best scan-able principle is to "colorize." Here's where you may need to learn how to do this with your unique software program. Most allow you to add color to specific emails.

For example, you can colorize mail to you specifically, mail you are only "cc'd" on, mail from a certain person, etc.

#4 – The 3 "Fs" of E-mail – Filters, Flags, & Folders

These elements of email are probably no new news, but I take nothing for granted because similar to the attendees in my seminars, the readers of this book have varied technical and software knowledge.

I recommend you educate yourself on how your software program integrates these ideas.

Do you use flags? How are you currently using them?...to sort by subject?...level of urgency?....to follow up?...are they colored? Lots of strategies can be employed for effective management.

Do you use filters? Some people call filters, *rules & preferences.* The basic premise of filters is to set up an e-mail to circumvent the inbox and go directly into a designated folder. You can determine - if it's from this person, if it has this in the subject line, or even if it has these words in the content, go directly to "x" designated folder.

This option works with my digital mantra: **less clicks - less decisions.** If an e-mail is not in my inbox, it's one less to sort or move.

A Few Examples:

One of my seminar attendees worked on a huge business campus that had a cafeteria. Each day the cafeteria would send out an e-mail outlining the day's specials.

He set up a folder entitled Cafeteria, then set up a filter so the e-mail would go directly to that folder. If he was so inclined to eat there that day, he just checked the folder for the current day's menu. At the end of the week, he just emptied the folder with one click.

Another attendee was an HR Manager who regularly sent out surveys to her staff of 100. Rather than have all the responses continue to flood her inbox, she set up a folder labeled Survey X and set up a filter for the responses.

As responses continued to come in throughout the day, she just checked the number to the right of the folder. As e-mails were added to the folder, the number next to the folder continued to rise. I love that you can check a folder without ever opening it.

In reviewing just these few suggestions you can find your 1%: sorting quickly, using filters, flags or folders, sorting quickly into temporary holding folders, purging daily or just sort and contain.

#5 - Consider more than 1 e-mail account

For those of you who are able to consider this, another way of automatic sorting (and having less clicks and decisions) is having more than one e-mail account.

Now you might think, "Oh my gosh this is one more thing to check." Not really–ever heard of a dashboard? Of course you have, you have one in your car! There is such a thing as a *digital dashboard* and it's a place where you can house all of your e-mail accounts and have them all at one glance. At the time of this writing, Yahoo has that capability.

Additionally, Gmail allows you to send multiple accounts to one primary Gmail account and have them automatically sorted into designated folders. This also honors the digital management principle of *less clicks – less decision*s and an earlier organizational principle of "all in one place."

#6 - Use Autoresponders

I really believe auto responders are underused. They are commonly known as the *out-of-office* reply. But out-of-office is just one use of the autoresponder. How might you use the autoresponder differently?

Here's an example: You have blocked out time to work on a critical report. Why not turn on your autoresponder and say, "I will not be checking or responding to email from 2pm-3pm. You can expect a response after 3:30 pm today."

#7 – Check your e-mail at fixed times of the day

Here's a great tip for those who are *not* e-mail driven in their work environments. Too many people disrupt their productivity with the excessive checking of email. Consider this tip from the book *The Four Hour Work Week* by Tim Ferris – check your e-mail at 11 am & 4 pm.

The theory is this. In a typical white-collar workday, most people are in their office generally between 8 and 9. People come in, they look at their first wave of e-mail, they respond. In general, the first wave of responses hits your in-box by 11.

So you check your mail, you do your responses, and then what happens with most people? They go to lunch. They come back. For many the first thing they do when they return from lunch is check their e-mail. That's when the second wave of responses goes out and arrives collectively in your in-box by 4 pm.

I tested this and found it to be generally true. Consider how you might use this. Even employing this practice a few days a week could impact your productivity over the course of a week.

Closing Question: What ideas or practices will you adopt for better email management?

✎ Notes

Section 4

Managing Time, Priorities, & Tasks

"It's not time management – it's life management.

Time is your life!"

Managing Time, Priorities, & Tasks

The Heart of Getting Results

Do you believe that one of the most precious, if not *the* most precious commodity you have is time?

Just hearing the phrase time management suggests it's something out there – separate from us. Yet it is us. It is your life. As I once read, "Life is a not a dress rehearsal, it's the only one you got."

Just the incredible thought that once a minute or a moment is gone it can't be retrieved puts into perspective how important this topic is. *So here are some key questions to consider:*

How do you want to spend (or use) your "life-time"?

How much are you letting other people spend your time?

Are you more active or passive in how you work with time?

Are you mindful of time?

What do you deeply desire your life to be and/or look like?.. to accomplish at work?

Are you aware of how your choices in the course of a day impact time both immediately and into the future?

How is your current time management impacting the perception of your work performance?...your actual results?

Some of these questions suggest that "life planning" may well be worth the investment of time as well as creating a mission statement. (By the way, some people call creating a vision board a form of life planning).

When I conduct career planning workshops I say that we spend more time planning our retirement, which we spend less of our lives in than we do planning our careers, which we spend the majority of our time in… and less time planning the whole of our lives.

Now, I know we can't control all of what happens in our life per se….but we can influence it more specifically if we are conscious of what we really want. In effect, **a decision is an act of control and influence.**

No matter what format you choose to use, I do recommend taking the time to disconnect yourself from your current every day schedule and contemplate the questions provided above.

Those answers offer you the opportunity to begin to live more intentionally and that can lead to a more satisfying life – *from the inside out.*

Additionally, though I won't address life planning, whatever answers you generate, will be the bull's-eye you'll want to hit and fuel the motivation needed to use the principles in this section.

This section is about how to hit the bulls-eye as much as possible, particularly in the area of work performance and getting intended results.

So, I'm sure you'll agree, **managing time is one of *the* most important skills to develop**; though I'm sure you've come to learn in reading this book that managing time is more about managing ourselves and the elements of life in the context of time.

I'm going to lay out a step by step process that is flexible but contains core principles and practices in effectively managing time.

As we begin this section, you'll notice that priorities and tasks are listed together in the subject heading; you'll see why as we go through the methods and principles.

Additionally, this section will not address long-term planning. It is about short-term planning within a cycle of a month.

Also, consider these principles for both your home and work life. For many readers, I recommend planning both together since work and personal time is so integrated.

We're going to start off with a mantra I recommend you memorize, **"Plan it - Map it - Manage it!"** This is the core process for effective time management and getting results.

PLAN IT

Do you plan?

Step 1: Set aside time to plan

Franklin Covey did a survey a few years back and asked this question, "How many of you plan your work week?" The answer...drum role please...32%.

I actually think that's pretty low. Do you believe that planning could help you get more desired results?...even 1% more? Not only do I believe it, I've experienced it.

Please know, I ask that question mindful of the fact that not everyone has 100% complete control over all of his or her time. Yet, with effective, strategic planning, time can be managed more successfully.

So when you plan, do so when you are not stressed and can think clearly.

When you plan is a personal preference. I usually start planning on Wednesday or Thursday for the upcoming week. Some I know plan on Monday of the week that is being planned. For sure, when planning becomes a part of your routine, the *when* will fall into place for you naturally and a personal planning rhythm will be created.

Step 2: Begin with a view of what's due.

Awe that has a nice ring to it doesn't it. This means look at a month at glance and get a sense of what's due in the course of the upcoming month.

If you don't already, I suggest you have deadlines written on or plugged into your calendar.

From a metaphoric perspective *getting a view of what's due* is like seeing the forest. I believe effective time management – getting the right results is creating the ability to consistently balance seeing both the forest and the trees. The commitment and rhythm of planning will help you do that.

Step 3: Work from and view your master task (or to do) list

So do you use a master list? What was one of the organizational principles that you learned earlier?...*all in one place.* That's one of the essential principles in using a master list. Here's why:

1. When you have a master list you have points of comparison. Points of comparison helps you make better decisions.

2. Things are less likely to fall through the cracks.

Some people are ruled by their list. It stresses them out if they can't complete it and some get overwhelmed just looking at it.

So for those who need to, let's reframe it and call it a **Master Tracking List.** Just using the word tracking suggests the purpose of the list is for something different - not necessarily to complete, but to keep track.

It also suggests that it will be ongoing, something that will be added to on a regular basis. This way your mind does not think that it will come to an end and create a stressful expectation of completion.

To increase achieving desired results, you'll want to use this approach - *track your work activity that then turns into actionable "to dos."* Go from "tasks to track."

Step 4: Determine your "A" absolutes

The next step is to indentify from your Master List the items that *absolutely* need to get done within the week or next.

By the way, notice I didn't say identify your "Bs and Cs." There is a reason for that. You'll notice as we work through the upcoming planning and mapping techniques you'll only have time for your A-absolutes.

I've discovered that in many cases the Bs percolate to As or drop off as well as the Cs. Or…it's taken care of by someone else. I say that is the universe working in your favor…isn't that wonderful!

Additionally, as you work through the rest of the steps in the Plan It, Map It, Manage it mantra, you'll discover you will only have time for the "As" anyway.

> To comprehend a man's life, it is necessary to know not merely what he does but also what he purposely leaves undone. There is a limit to the work that can be got out of a human body or a human brain, and he is a wise man who wastes no energy on pursuits for which he is not fitted; and he is still wiser who, from among the things that he can do well, chooses and resolutely follows the best.
> **John Hall Gladstone**

What's constitutes an "A – Absolute"?

In order to determine your A-absolutes, I recommend you use the questions provided below as starters. You may need to add more unique to your needs.

In the case when really tight competing priorities are on your list, create a checklist grid and attribute numerical value to each question. You'll be able to add all the numbers. The ones with the highest score will qualify as your absolutes. In many cases, the questions alone will assist your decision-making without the need for the grid.

Questions to Determine Your "A" Absolutes:

1 – When does it absolutely need to get done?...meaning the factual deadline, not the assumed one.

What do I mean by that? Let's go back to e-mail. Someone sends you an e-mail that says I need blank, but they didn't give you a time or date. How do you prioritize it?

In some cases, you'll need to ask for a date and time. And frankly, I think it improves productivity collectively in a group, when you work with factual – tangible deadlines.

In one of my seminars there was a discussion about *soft deadlines vs. hard deadlines*. I think sometimes soft deadlines actually make you more unproductive; in effect making it more difficult to make effective decisions.

I recommend you work with hard deadlines. The better phrase is due date. A date is a fixed time.

2 – Is someone waiting for it? Sometimes you might be procrastinating with something where somebody's actually waiting for something.

3 – How does this relate to my boss's values or expectations?

4 – Who is waiting for it?

5 – Who gave it to me?

6 - What are the consequences if it doesn't get done?

When looking at the consequences, think of it in these four contexts: what's the consequence to me; what's the consequence to the team or department; what's the consequence to my boss; and what's the consequence to the overall company objectives or objectives of the project.

7 – How much does it bug me? Why is this an important question?

Here's an example: If you're walking down the street and you've got a pebble in your shoe, are you going to keep walking or are you going to take it out? You're going to take it out. Why?...it'll hurt, cause you to bleed and impede your ability to smoothly get you to where you want to go.

The same holds true if something is bugging you. Ok, you're not going to bleed, but it can impede productivity. I call it eliminating the "monkey on your back," or the distracter. The distracter could cause mistakes on more important tasks. Additionally, it may not qualify for questions 1 - 6, but does qualify for #7.

So get rid of it, clear your mind, and free up your motivation and energy.

Those are the questions that I recommend using to decide your A-Absolutes.

Consider how else or with whom you could use these questions? What else could you use them for?

You could use the list to coach other people. Let's say someone comes to you and they're acting like something is a crisis. You can ask them these questions to help them figure out where it fits in the scheme of things and determine if it's a legitimate fire.

This also is a great list to use with your boss when sorting through ad hoc stuff being added throughout the week. If you can ask questions to help to prioritize, that indirectly coaches others to be more strategic in how they view work and it helps create a collaborative approach.

And for those of you who tend to say, "yes" too soon, you can rely on the questions rather than regret or resent it later.

These questions are a great resource for tactfully managing others, as well as your own work.

MAP IT – Create a Time Map

This time management technique and practice is very powerful and dare I say life changing. Your goal is to **create a time-map** of your intended, desired activity/results for the week. What's the fundamental purpose of a map?...to give you direction on how to get to a desired destination.

> *I recommend you take care of the minutes and the hours will take care of themselves.*
> - Earl of Chesterfield

In using a time map, here is the key: go from being list orientated to being schedule - time orientated.

In doing so, you're going to work from *a week-at-a-glance.* Personally, I use and print off an Excel version, but it can be done with or on any calendaring system.

The essence of time mapping is to plug your "A-absolutes" into your calendar – that is make an appointment with them using the following **time mapping practices.** (Here is where the strategic thinking kicks in again):

Time Mapping Practices

1- Time Estimation – estimate how long you want to spend on each item or how long you think it will take to do. Please note (and this is THE most important point of this section) <u>most people have no idea how long things take to do.</u>

Because of this, there are lots of unrealistic expectations about how and when work should get done. If this is true, undue stress is being created because of **time distortion.**

Another component of time distortion is stress related. The more negative stress someone feels, the more distorted is their sense of time.

As mentioned in an earlier section, imagine when people are creating expectations and deadlines, and are doing so in time distortion, coupled with the fact that they don't know how long something takes to do. The result is just stress on top of stress. By the way, time distortion is one of the key reasons for planning when you're calm and your mind is clear.

So, if you don't know how long your tasks will take, if time estimation is new to you – the rule of thumb is *to estimate how long you think it will take and double it.*

Time estimation helps you build and nurture time awareness. You must be time aware to skillfully manage time.

Create a list both for home and work of commonly performed tasks and how long each takes. For example: how long does it take to do a load of laundry, fill up the gas tank, pay bills, execute an invoice, sort through your e-mail.

The more you know factually, the better you will be at realistically managing your time, developing the skill of time mapping and minimizing the stress surrounding it.

2- Time Block - block out time for each activity in your calendar. Here's where you'll plug into your calendar what activities or tasks you'll do when.

3 - Consider your P.P.P. - Peak Productivity Period. While deciding when you'll do something, keep in mind your peak period. (I also call it being in "the zone.")

Why? Well think for a moment what qualities you're experiencing during your peak period?

Name some....

Focused, motivated, better - clearer decision-making, more creative, positive, perhaps more willing to do something you don't like, probably make less mistakes, efficient.

Consider this list of characteristics your productivity gold! In fact, consider them your human resource! Please...I'm begging you...don't spend it on coffee talk or water cooler conversations. Guard that time – be vigilant in its usage.

An additional reason why considering your peak period when mapping out your tasks is critical is the Pareto's Principle (also known as the 80/20 rule). Named after the Italian economist Alfredo Pareto, he observed in 1906 that 80% of the land in Italy was owned by 20% of the population.

How does that relate to your productivity? Here's what the 80/20 rule suggests: 20% of your concentrated effort gets 80% of your needed, desired results. So to take advantage of this theory, you'll want to make sure that your most important activities (A-absolutes) are plugged into your most productive time. Applying this tip alone could give you your 1%. Imagine if an entire team applied it!

The Pareto's Principle

This principle is a widely accepted one as noted below. The distribution shows up in several different aspects relevant to entrepreneurs and business managers. For example:

- 80% of your profits come from 20% of your customers
- 80% of your complaints come from 20% of your customers
- 80% of your profits come from 20% of the time you spend
- 80% of your sales come from 20% of your products
- 80% of your sales are made by 20% of your sales staff

Therefore, many businesses have easy access to dramatic improvements in profitability by focusing on the most effective areas and eliminating, ignoring, automating, delegating or re-training the rest, as appropriate.

Source:
http://en.wikipedia.org/wiki/Pareto_principle

In working with your peak period considering the following:

There are **3 kinds of peaks**: biological (natural), environmental (meaning I can get more done when there are less people in the office), and conditioned (I do shift work and I am awake and productive at 12:00 midnight, though that is not natural for me).

Additionally, there is a **peak within a peak**. In any productivity cycle there is a ramp up period and a ramp down. I use this principle with tasks I may not genuinely like. I plug them into the peak of my peak – when I'm at the height of being the most naturally motivated, positive, and focused.

I need to mention I know not everyone even has complete control over his or her peak time. So again, I'll stress use these principles the best you can within your real contexts. Even a little usage of how you use your peak period can make a measureable difference.

Step 6: Negotiable or Non-negotiable

This mapping principle is as it sounds - is where you've placed the item on your time map negotiable or non-negotiable? Does this item need to stay where I've placed it or can it be bumped to another time. You can use these codes on your map - *"n or nn."*

This principle is really handy for shared calendaring when firmly securing time related to deadlines and for ensuring things will not fall through the cracks.

This is also great for shared calendaring, when colleagues are trying to capture time for meetings and also helps manage their perception of how you're using your work time.

Stop & Consider...

Before we move on you might be noticing that after time mapping – plugging into your calendar your to do activities combined with conference calls and meetings - how little time you have left. And, you've yet to plug in checking e-mails, sorting through papers, and other routine activities.

In reality, most of us are lucky if we can just get our A-absolutes done! **And here in lies a major point and benefit of working with these principles and methods – you work from reality.** Time mapping - being schedule orientated vs. list orientated - helps you be more grounded in real time. This way of working helps you more effectively manage expectations and ultimately your stress.

Additionally, concrete knowledge of time will assist you in being more strategic and vigilant with your usage of time, negotiate your yes and no's with more confidence, and communicate more outside the context of emotions.

Consider for a moment: How will this time management technique help *you*?

Benefits & Use of a Time Map

☺ *Performance Management Strategy: Under-promise, over-deliver*

A promise is an expectation. A promise means I'm going to get it done.

When we function in time distortion, many times we will *over promise* because we do not have a realistic sense of time.

Additionally, this is also where personality plays a role; if you are a spontaneous decision maker you might say yes too quickly or if you have the desire to please and get along, you might agree to something only to regret or resent it later.

The way to help manage all that more effectively is by being aware of your tendencies and making a point to use your map as a discussion tool.

This strategy will also serve to reduce your stress. <u>You've got to know how long things take to do and work from a schedule.</u>

☺ *Helps you stay on track even when you're interrupted.*

Unanticipated things will surface. You're going to have detours. That's absolutely the truth. What productivity experts say, is when you get taken off task and then come back to your space, the first thing you say is, " Now, where was I?" If you've got a lot on your desk, and you don't have a map, you might pick up the less than best thing just to feel like you're starting to do something and then the more important items may fall through the cracks.

How does a map help you with that? You know where you left off. A map is something you can pick up and begin driving again.

Remember, that map was made when you were not stressed and clearer in your thinking.

☺ Tracks your performance

Some people are asked to do their own performance reviews. Is that true for you? Bless your heart; I can't remember what I did yesterday let alone for a whole year, and that is the point. What does mapping help you do?

Though you are tracking time, you are also tracking your performance. Is that a good thing? You want to negotiate or make a case for a raise? You've got credible information you need to have the discussion. Do you have multiple projects that you've devoted a certain allotment of time to? Now you'll be able to offer clear numbers.

By the way, as a career coach, I think people greatly under value and under state what they've done in a performance review because they can't remember the whole of a years experience.

✍*Helps in negotiating increased or decreased work load*

Let's say your boss comes up to you and says, "I need for you to do this, this and this." Your response, "Okay, I'm happy to take it on. (Now physically you have a map in front of you) and say, " Okay, this is what I have mapped out for the week, what do you want me to bump?"

It's a wonderful tool to have a tangible, collaborative conversation in real time. Additionally consider it a tool to help *train your boss and team members* to think more practically and concretely about time. Help them build time awareness too. Remember, most people have no idea how long things take to do and therefore set unrealistic expectations.

Key Tip: I recommend having your map with you at meetings, lay it out on your desk or cube area for colleagues to see when they walk in. Talk and work from it regularly. Educate colleagues by how you conduct yourself throughout the workday. Let them know that you are very time aware and that you want them to be respectful of your time as you are respectful of theirs.

I had a client who said to me, "JoAnn, I just think I'm in too many interdepartmental meetings." I said, "Do you know that for a fact or do you just feel that way?" He said, "I feel that way and it is a fact." I said, "Okay, prove it to me. He said, "I can't."

I said, "The best thing you can do is to be able to prove it to your boss." So for one quarter he mapped out where his time went. The results of that exercise even shocked him.

He discovered that he was in interdepartmental meetings 30% of his work time. He met with his boss and his boss responded just as he thought - proclaimed he was in too many meetings. They came up with a strategy to obtain needed information, which greatly reduced his attendance.

The results? The next quarter his productivity went up 25% and all that was a result of following one simple practice - time mapping! I call that the power of 1%!

Having that map, again presented the opportunity for a much better professional conversation than walking in and presenting vague information.

Important question: In what other ways can a time map be useful to you?…to your team?...for your boss?

Notes

Manage It

The final piece of our time management mantra is - Manage It! The follow up principle is to **plan by the week and manage by the day.** Here's where your mapping will be tweaked throughout the week. In some cases you'll need to manage by the hours.

> In summary the real key to these time, task, & priorities techniques is go from being list oriented to being schedule – time oriented.

I recommend first thing in the morning or before you leave the night before, look at your map and as things evolve in your work week, update your map.

As you move throughout the day, your priorities may be shifting regularly. You'll need to have updated conversations with people. You'll have to manage how you work with and negotiate "fires" with the "A-Absolute" list questions. You'll have to manage interruptions and the day-to-day give and take of your collaborative work flow as it reflects on your map.

Note: Notice how many times I used the word manage.

Consider this - my calendar is my left hand and my master tracking list is my right hand. They can't function without each other and sometimes you will use them interchangeably. For example, if a tight deadline action comes up, you can skip the list and put it straight on your schedule.

Also in the spirit of "manage it", I want to address three of the most popular needs that are discussed in my seminars that relate to this section of "managing it".

Procrastination, Perfectionism, & Interruptions

Rather than go into great detail explaining them, most people know exactly what they are, so I'll just give you my favor tips for addressing them.

Procrastination

I think there are 3 major reasons why procrastination happens:

1. People put off doing tasks they don't genuinely enjoy. Remember the TFDB formula? If there is no pleasure, some will put if off. Why...because if you loved it...you'd be doing it. Most people don't put off doing things they genuinely enjoy.
2. They make the task bigger in their minds than what it really it.
3. For left brainers – they feel if they can't do it right, why attempt it at all right now.

Here is one of my favorite tips and it's housed in a personal confession.

Tip: **The One Minute Challenge**

The goal of the one minute challenge is to work with the 4 "M's."

Minute, Motivation, Momentum, Music

Context Example: A chore I don't like

I have to admit that cleaning house is one of my least favorite life tasks. My idea of cleaning house is sweeping the room with a glance. Unfortunately, that doesn't catch the dust bunnies.

And, according to my mom it started very young. She informed me one day that I had proclaimed at the age of six that was going to become an executive and hire a maid. Where did I get that from at the age of six?

Anyway I have used the one minute challenge to overcome my procrastination in this area and trick myself into sustained action. (Yes sometimes we have to resort to tricking ourselves).

Additionally this tip works with a key brain function – the release of chemicals. As mentioned in the *Me in Team* section, negative stress releases Cortisol. This chemical actual demotivates. It causes you to feel tired. So this tip encourages "motivating chemicals" as well.

One of the quickest ways I have found to quickly release pleasurable – motivating chemicals is to listen to music.

So let's say I have to sweep the kitchen. I get out my kitchen timer, and I say, "JoAnn, you only have to do it for one minute. Now I think, oh, for one minute I can do that." But, I have to have a little help. So one of my favorite "clean-to music" songs is James Brown's *I Got That Feeling*.

So imagine, I've got my broom. I got my dustpan. I turn on a little James and I start feeling the beat of the music – "I got that feeling, baby" and I'm starting to jam, getting in the groove - the broom and me are dancing. And before you know it, I'm so into the music, I don't even hear the timer go off. I got five minutes of sweeping kicked out. And I feel so jazzed.

This is one of the most effective ways to jump start motivation and gain momentum when you have to do something you don't find pleasurable.

It is a great self-coaching technique with a science behind it; it works with your brain chemistry. With this tip, you're connecting the work to the feeling of the music. That's called an anchor in the world of NLP (neural linguistic programming).

Perfectionism

As mentioned in a previous section, those who are dominate left brain have a tendency towards this behavior the most.

Also from a personality standpoint, those who have a need to "get it right" tend to struggle with this as well. They have a need to have it right not only for themselves, but right in how it's seen by others. Because of that, they can get caught up in the paralysis of analysis and pushing to the edge of deadlines, which can generate stress to themselves and other team members.

My favorite tip: When generating work product, use the phrase **First Draft.**

When you hear that phrase, what comes to mind? I interpret that phrase to mean, not perfect or completely correct the first time around. Mistakes or corrections are to be expected.

The irony for folks who need to use *first draft* to let go of something and not work endlessly on it is… their first draft is probably going to be much better than everybody else's 4th or 5th!

Tracking Your Results – A Career Success Strategy

I really think it's important to track your performance / productivity. Even when doing a resume, I ask clients to quantitate how they are contributing to a company. Quantitate means providing numbers or percentages in terms of how you describe your performance.

Use your map to send reports to your manager of the things you actually got done. Here are my results for the week. Or, I spent this much time on Project A.

Additionally, you might want to consider the word results vs. goal and in doing so ask yourself this questions, "What are the results I want today?"

Notice when you use the word result. It has a whole different impact on your brain and your thinking than goal. When I use it, it puts me in a different state of mind. The word *result* feels more concrete to me; it has a more action oriented feel and is very empowering. Consider thinking in terms of results.

Life Success

Sidebar

The Power of Now

In Time Management

*"I do believe that living an empowered and successful life **now** is grounded in being aware of the opportunity for choosing in each moment."*

You may be familiar with this phrase. Several years ago a book was released by Ekhart Tolle entitled *The Power of Now*. Interesting read I must say.

One of many takeaways from that book is thinking about the concept of "now."…as opposed to earlier or later.

I think for many (and I'm including myself in this) we think in terms of what's coming up vs. focusing on what's happening at the moment primarily because we have so much going on. It might be described as partially functioning in the present while constantly anticipating the future. And because of that, we are rarely if ever *all in the moment.*

So if it's even remotely true that we are rarely all in the moment, are we at our best in our moments? Can we give our best in a moment when we portioning part of ourselves out in anticipating the future? Why does this matter? It matters because a moment is a segment of time. A moment turns into minutes, which turns into weeks, months, years….a life time.

Can we conclude then, that not maximizing our moments, giving our best in a moment undermines living an empowered life now? What a thought – the "nows" formulate a life time. Ah ha! That's where that phrase, "being in the moment" comes from.

At this point, probably some questions on how can we live more in the moment are appropriate.

Should we....slow down, become more aware, focus on 1 task or event at a time?

Perhaps our mantra really should be "map by the week and manage by moments..."

You decide.

One Additional Consideration

In order to accomplish any of this we need to consider another element in living an empowered life now and that is choice. Each moment is presented with a choice. A choice is defined as "*actively* choosing." Making a choice is exerting power. Each choice generates a result. Each result is a building block of our life.

Conscious choosing is empowering and we feel more of a sense of ownership to the results generated.

I also believe that in not doing that, we may begin to feel and take on a disempowered victim role where we might interpret life as happening to us rather than seeing ourselves as participating in life and doing all *we* can.

Managing Interruptions

We train people how to treat us.

If you don't like the way you're being treated, ask yourself, "What am I allowing and why...or what about me is allowing this to happen?"

We are in the age of the "sort of open door policy." Or I call it "open cube." It's saying, "I'm available, but not really."

In fact there are more and more companies that are doing away with offices and in the spirit of "collaboration" designing open workspaces. There is a lot I could say about that, but I'll leave that to a blog post. For now I'll state that design is not always the best for every team member and may create the opposite outcome...more stress, harder to be productive, etc.

Additionally, in some contexts interruptions have to happen (working on a project deadline) or it's built into someone's job description (receptionist). *The key is managing them successfully based on the reality of your work needs.*

The fact that we are expected to be more available than ever also commands a need to be very skilled at managing interruptions with tact and finesse!

There are many ideas on how to manage interruptions, yet I want to share with you my favorite because the technique communicates a lot in addition to being an effective time management - productivity practice.

The overall tip is to **lead with your body while setting boundaries.** Here is the step-by-step how-to:

Step 1 - Stand up

When someone enters your workspace (cube or office) immediately stand up. The bottom line?...you're communicating, "Don't get comfortable – yet I can talk for a moment." You could even move toward the opening of your cube. If you're in an office, consider meeting them in front of your desk, or as I say in my seminars, "Head 'em off at the pass."

This particular tip has great value because it can communicate other things as well. It can be perceived as a sign of respect, you're face to face reflecting your full attention, it suggests power and initiating control, and I'm sure you can name more.

Step 2 - State a time limit boundary.

This is taking control and the lead in letting someone know how you want to handle the interruption. Some people don't do that and then get angry when people continue to talk longer than what feels acceptable. That's called passive aggressive behavior, by the way. It's being angry for having a boundary violated without ever communicating what the boundary was in the first place.

> **Power tip:**
> **Someone is leading someone.**
>
> Are they leading you or are you leading them? When it comes to your space and time, you need to be the leader of that…you are responsible for those personal assets – space, time, and attention.

Using your own personality style, say something like, "Hi, what can I help you with, I only have three minutes right now." Consider the time limit of 3 or 5. The key is to state a <u>specific and limited time frame</u>.

I recommend not saying, "a few." I'm sure you've experienced a few minutes turning into many.

Additional phrases you could use are: "You have my full attention for the next 3 minutes." Or, "I'm all yours for 3 minutes."

Why three? In testing this, here's what you'll discover. Generally speaking, three minutes is enough time to answer a question, determine if it's a legitimate need that needs attention right now, or it's something that's important but can be scheduled for an additional conversation at another time.

Please note: If people are not use to you doing this – they may be taken back. So delivery is everything – it's all in the tone!

Step 3 - Look at a time piece

Why? It sends this message to an interrupter's brain, "He/she really is serious about the three minutes."

Some of my coaching clients try to make it fun. One of them uses a sand timer from a board game. When people come into her office, they voluntarily turn over the timer. They know they have to be quick and specific because they only have the sand to work with.

One of many great benefits of this approach is her staff has been trained to communicate more effectively and have built sensitivity to being respectful of each other's time.

Step 4 – Close the time with a prepared closing statement

Make sure you maintain the leadership mode by *not expecting them* to close the conversation. You must be prepared and expect yourself to do so.

The best way to be prepared is to *have some pre-scripted statements* that you feel comfortable delivering. Scripting helps you be clear and comfortable. Here is also where the tact and finesse comes in; word and tone are important especially depending on the employee's personality and that of your boss as well. All these considerations will make it much easier to execute.

The easiest closing statement is when it's clear further discussion is needed. All that needs to be said is, "How about you e-mail me a couple times you're available and we'll schedule a time to continue this discussion." Notice the strategy is to ask them to take action; it's a delegated action.

Additional statements could begin this way:

"how about you…"

"I've got to get back to …"

"I know you've got to get back to….and so do I."

"I know you're busy, so I'll …"

Or…create & script your own…

Notice these are either I statements or you statements.

"I know <u>you're</u> working on a tight deadline, so I'll let <u>you</u> get back to you it.

<u>I'm</u> working on a tight deadline, so <u>I</u> need to get back to…"

Tip: You may need to have customized statements for specific people.

SPECIAL NOTE: There will be some people that no matter how gracious you try to be, they will not read your clues. So know that you will need to be firm and strong in how you execute these 4 steps. They will need to feel your **confident, directive** energy. And in some cases you will have to say your closing statement, turn your back and/or walk away.

Additionally, be armed with the attitude that you have graciously given **your time** and they need to respect the boundaries you've expressed!

A Few Additional Interruption Tips:

- Don't have any chairs in your work area
- Put something personal in a chair – people tend to hesitate touching personal items.

⌂ Notes

Tips For A Team

Honestly, the best way to manage interruptions is doing it within the context of the entire team. It's part of and an understanding within a team culture.

Another client wanted to manage interruptions from a team perspective. Someone came up with the idea of using a stop light concept. So everyone designed and decorated their own and placed them outside of their office or cube.

Everyone gets the message based on the color just like the traffic stoplight; it's green for c'mon in, red for don't, and yellow for proceed with caution.

Additionally, some people have a small whiteboard or box outside their space where those stopping by can just place a message or documents with notes.

This, by the way, is a great way of gaining the 1% for an entire team.

Use S.W.A.T.s

Another fun and high-mileage solution for team time management is an activity called SWATs. A S.W.A.T. is a 7 to 10 minute standup meeting (usually in a circle). It stands for Short, Worthwhile, Appointed, Time, and can be done as frequently as needed - perhaps twice or even three times a week.

It's a short meeting where everybody gets face time, sees what's on the plate of fellow team members, improves the communication of members, and everybody leaves feeling connected.

To execute it at a minimum all you need really is a facilitator and a timekeeper. And by the way, the facilitator should not always be the manager. Everybody should have a chance. The Timekeeper keeps track of how long people talk and the length of the meeting. Also, it's best to conduct it standing up.

Some of my clients have taken it to a whole new level. They like to have an inspirational quote. Some enjoy giving out recognitions and award. Walmart calls them huddles. I've walk in early in the morning and witnessed a cheer and singing.

It is a great way to manage workloads, keep everyone in the know of who needs help with what, develop a "let's help each other environment" and create public accountability for getting results.

It's a collaborative, interactive, and motivating activity. Skies the limit in terms of how to leverage this idea to increase team productivity and nurture a positive team culture.

Conclusion

As this section closes, I want to end with a wonderful antidotal story that really sums it all up.

Rocks – A Science Lesson on Life's Priorities

One day, an expert in time management was speaking to a group of business students and to drive home a point, used an illustration those students will never forget.

As he stood in front of the group of high-powered overachievers, he said," Okay, time for a quiz." He then pulled out a one-gallon, wide-mouthed mason jar and set it on the table in front of him.

Then he produced about a dozen fist-sized rocks and carefully placed them one by one, into the jar. When the jar was filled to the top and no more rocks would fit inside, he asked, "Is this jar full?" Everyone in the class said, "Yes."

Then he said, "Really?" He reached under the table and pulled out a bucket of gravel. Then he dumped some gravel in and shook the jar, causing pieces of gravel to work themselves down into the space between the big rocks.

Then he asked the group once more. "Is this jar full?" By this time the class was on to him. "Probably not," one of them answered. "Good!" He replied. He reached under the table and brought out a bucket of sand. He started dumping the sand into the jar and it went into all the spaces left between the rocks and the gravel. Once more he asked the question. "Is this jar full?" "No!" the class shouted. Once again, he said "Good."

Then he grabbed a pitcher of water and began to pour it until the jar was filled to the brim.

Then the expert in time-management looked at the class and asked, "What is the point of this illustration?" One eager beaver raised his hand and said, "The point is, no matter how full your schedule is, if you try really hard you can always fit some more things in it." "NO," the speaker replied, "That's not the point."

The truth this illustration teaches us is this: If you don't put the big rocks in first, you'll never get them in at all. So, what are the big rocks in your life?...your children, your loved ones, your education, your dreams, a worthy cause, teaching or mentoring others, doing things that you love, time for yourself, your health, your significant other. Remember to put these BIG ROCKS in first, or you'll never get them in at all."

If you sweat the little stuff (i.e. the gravel, the sand) then you'll fill your life with little things you worry about that don't really matter, and you'll never have the real quality time and energy you need to spend on the big important stuff - the big rocks.

Tonight, or in the morning, when you are reflecting on this short story, ask yourself this question:

What are the "big rocks" in my life? Then, put those in your jar first.

From My Heart

I really hope the content of this book has aided you just a bit more in managing your big rocks.

JoAnn

"If it will be, it's up to me."

Cindy Kubica

Closing Thoughts

"Being in control of your life and having realistic expectations about your day-to-day challenges are the keys to stress management, which is perhaps the most important ingredient to living a happy, healthy and rewarding life."

-Marilu Henner

I'm sure you've found lots of ideas and strategies on how to manage time, priorities, people, and information so that they or it does not manage you, but you are managing it!

Remember time is *your life!* Ultimately this book was written in an effort to serve you in getting results and by that creating the life you really want though the lens of time, organization, and priority management.

As I close, I really want to stress - focus on just one thing to start with. That one thing could make all the difference! Consider this example:

After I present the managing interruption tips in my seminar, I pose this question, "How much time do you think you could recapture in a day from that one tip?" I get a myriad of answers ranging from several hours to 15 – 20 minutes.

I then ask them to calculate the answer using numbers on the low side, so we usually use 30 minutes. Here's how it looks:

1 Week: 30 mins. a day recaptured x 5 days = 150 mins. (2.5 hrs.)

1 Month: 150 mins. x 4 weeks = 600 mins. (10 hrs)

1 Quarter: 10 hrs. in a month x 3 mths. = 30 hrs (3.75 days assuming 8 hrs in an average work day).

1 Year: 30 hrs x 4 quarters = 120 hrs. (15 days divided by 5 work days = **3 weeks!**

Think about it for a moment - taking back 3 weeks of time!! Now, calculate that for an entire team. How could that impact a company's bottom line?

This is the power of 1 – This is finding the 1%!

Getting Support – Individual Coaching, A Blog, or Seminars

I think it bears repeating again that just because someone has read something doesn't mean they can or will implement it.

Coaching…

With that in mind, if you find yourself stuck or in need of help implementing the tips and strategies, don't hesitate to contact me at http://www.joanncorley.com. Because you have bought this book, you are entitled to a free coaching call.

Blog...

Also, in the spirit of the new book publishing model, join the conversation in gaining and keeping your 1% edge at www.the1percentedge.com. Subscribe to this blog or join me on other social media mediums to get value added tips and notices regarding webinars and other learning offerings.

Or, send me an email and share with me your progress. I'd love to hear from you: joann@joanncorley.com

Live Seminar...

And finally, if you feel this book has helped you, consider bringing or referring the companion workshop to your company or professional association. You can contact me via the above referenced websites or email me at joann@joanncorley.com.

To your success and happiness!

Your portable coach,

JoAnn

About the Author

People have said about JoAnn that she is "an emerging voice to be heard in the business marketplace"...a catalyst for innovative thinking...passionate for bringing theory into reality in the laboratory of real life!

She brings fresh thinking that matches the realistic career and management needs of the 21st century workplace and can be seen in print publications and heard on radio shows across the country.

JoAnn Corley is a dynamic, inspiring speaker, trainer, career and management coach. She has a contagious passion and energy for the topics she teaches and has shared that passion with thousands across North America specializing in seminars on getting results, creative and innovative thinking, effective management and leadership, communication & collaboration and dynamic team synergy & productivity.

She is contributing author to the book, Ordinary Women, Extraordinary Success, a collaborative effort with some of the top female motivational speakers in North American and hailed by Jack Canfield of Chicken Soup for the Soul fame as a must read, Wisdom@Work and The 1% Edge – Power Strategies to Increase Your Management Effectiveness.

She founded her human resource-organizational development firm in 1998, which has provided services to a variety of industries. JoAnn utilizes her 20+ years of business experience, expertise in the knowledge of work functions and thousands of hours of human behavior coaching to consult in a variety of areas.

She took her consulting and coaching experience on the road conducting seminars and workshops all over North America and Puerto Rico. She has spoken to thousands of people and in every major city in the U.S.

Companies whose employees have experienced JoAnn's dynamic workshops include: The City of Chicago, U.S. Marshals Service, Microsoft, 3M Corporation, Trump Enterprises, NASA, University of Texas, and the U.S. Army, Fort Hood, TX, The Chicago White Sox, Duke University, The Yale Club, New York, HBO, ESPN to name a very few.

Ms. Corley attended Concordia College, Moorhead, MN and Eastern Illinois University. Prior to launching her consulting practice, she spent several years as an International Benefits Manager as well as a Senior Recruiter for a Chicago recruiting firm. She is currently a member of S.H.R.M., A.S.T.D. and A.B.W.A.

Made in the USA
Charleston, SC
06 January 2012